Essays and Studies 1999

Series Editor: Gordon Campbell

The English Association

The objects of the English Association are to promote the knowledge and appreciation of the English language and its literature, and to foster good practice in its teaching and learning at all levels.

The association pursues these aims by creating opportunities of co-operation among all those interested in English; by furthering the recognition of English as essential in education; by discussing methods of English teaching; by holding lectures, conferences, and other meetings; by publishing journals, books, and leaflets; and by forming local branches.

Publications

The Year's Work in English Studies. An annual bibliography. Published by Blackwell.

The Year's Work in Critical and Cultural Theory. An annual bibliography. Published by Blackwell.

Essays and Studies. An annual volume of essays by various scholars assembled by the collector covering usually a wide range of subjects and authors from the medieval to the modern. Published by D. S. Brewer.

English. A journal of the Association, *English* is published three times a year by the Association.

The Use of English. A journal of the Association, *The Use of English* is published three times a year by the Association.

Newsletter. A *Newsletter* is published three times a year giving information about forthcoming publications, conferences, and other matters of interest.

Benefits of Membership

Institutional Membership

Full members receive copies of *The Year's Work in English Studies*, *Essays and Studies*, *English* (3 issues) and three *Newsletters*.

Ordinary Membership covers *English* (3 issues) and three *Newsletters*.

Schools Membership includes copies of each issue of *English* and *The Use of English*, one copy of *Essays and Studies*, three *Newsletters*, and preferential booking and rates for various conferences held by the Association.

Individual Membership

Individuals take out Basic Membership, which entitles them to buy all regular publications of the English Association at a discounted price, and attend Association gatherings.

For further details write to The Secretary, The English Association, The University of Leicester, University Road, Leicester, LE1 7RH.

Essays and Studies 1999

Postcolonial Theory and Criticism

Edited by
Laura Chrisman and Benita Parry

for the English Association

D. S. BREWER

ESSAYS AND STUDIES 1999
IS VOLUME FIFTY-TWO IN THE NEW SERIES
OF ESSAYS AND STUDIES COLLECTED ON BEHALF OF
THE ENGLISH ASSOCIATION
ISSN 0071–1357

First published 2000
D. S. Brewer, Cambridge

D. S. Brewer is an imprint of Boydell & Brewer Ltd
PO Box 9, Woodbridge, Suffolk IP12 3DF, UK
and of Boydell & Brewer Inc.
PO Box 41026, Rochester, NY 14604–4126, USA
website: http: //www.boydell.co.uk

ISBN 0 85991 554 9

A catalogue record for this book is available
from the British Library

The Library of Congress has cataloged this serial publication:
Catalog card number 36–8431

This publication is printed on acid-free paper

Typeset by Joshua Associates Ltd, Oxford
Printed in Great Britain by
St Edmundsbury Press Ltd, Bury St Edmunds, Suffolk

Contents

Editors' Introduction

The range of this collection covers literary discussions of colonialist, modern anti-colonial and contemporary postcolonial writings; theoretical explorations of nineteenth-century imperialism and late twentieth-century neo-colonialism; the geo-political regions of Latin America, India, the Caribbean, the Pacific, Africa, Anglo-America and the United Kingdom. A number of concerns unify the essays, the most prominent being a commitment to ground the analysis of aesthetic culture in the historical, social and political realities of its production. Unremarkable in itself, this materialist approach has not been prevalent in the field of postcolonial cultural studies as practised within metropolitan academies, where a culturalist approach bypasses a consideration of material conditions, or else subsumes 'materiality' into 'textuality'.

In this volume contributors argue for an understanding of culture as materially produced and in certain situations utilised precisely to obscure or deflect awareness of material reality (Quayson, Phillips, Coronil). Hence the essays emphasise the need to foreground and extend the exploration of 'materiality', so that not only socio-economic, macrological processes but also the physical materiality of human bodies (Phillips), or the spatial materiality of domestic interiors and local environment (Sandhu, Quayson), are factored into the analysis. Addressing the role of physical illness in the writings of R.L. Stevenson and Jack London, Phillips approaches contagion and disease in the South Seas not only as metaphorical, but also as the material consequences of colonial expansionism. For Quayson, where theorists parallel sign systems with political processes, fiction and fact are put on the same footing, so that relations of power, social conflict and actual struggles against oppression and deprivation are occluded.

If the materialist orientation of this collection constitutes one of its distinctions, another is its regional scope. In the fields of colonial and postcolonial studies, Anglophone literary history has often operated without comparison to non-Anglophone experience. This model, however, is now being challenged, especially by Americanists and Africanists for whom the long historical legacy and (trans)continental reach of imperial expansionism makes an exclusively English language/ nation focus highly inappropriate. A number of the essays included here explicitly and implicitly argue for the extension of postcolonial theory and analysis to the Americas in ways which break down distinctions between 'North' and 'South' American, between English and Spanish expansionist history and culture (Cooppan, Coronil). In another comparativist register, an essay which recovers the importance of the South Seas for the formation of colonial identities (Phillips) enhances the undertanding of a period which all too often is conceptualised as one for which the 'new imperialism' in Africa, and the established imperialism in India, were the only expressions of British expansionism; while Watson's discussion of Kipling reveals that Kipling's India is informed by anxieties deriving from Irish as well as Indian nationalism.

Recognising that unrest and opposition were integral to British imperialism, contributors address the literary strategies devised by writers to contain the insecurities of empire. Thus Phillips shows that the paternalism and racial superiority inscribed by the British R.L. Stevenson and the American Jack London to exonerate imperial ventures is undermined by configurations of colonialism as parasitical and a carrier of pestilence. In his discussion of Kipling's India, Watson uncovers Kipling's attempts to translate imperial instabilities into strengths. A procedure calculated to deny what the empire knew to be its weakness generated a further paradox since Kipling, who hated the Irish independence movement, co-opted the 'common men' of this colonised people to police India, allotting these footsoldiers of British empire a loyalty and responsibility at variance with the treachery of their peers in Ireland.

A number of the studies stress the importance of reassessing nationalist–liberationist writings and attest to the oppositional power held by anti-colonial nationalist movements, a power that may be neglected today within postcolonial studies but was not ignored by imperial practices. Thus Cooppan urges the inclusion within postcolonial curriculae of theorists like the Cuban José Martí and the African-American W.E.B. Du Bois, advocating that such analysis should embrace not only their literary but also their polemic and sociological writings, not only the academic but the activist elements of their nationalism. Similarly Premnath argues for an understanding of Frantz Fanon that resituates his work within the decolonising project which animated his writing and which perceives his vision of national liberation movements as dialectical rather than linear or vanguardist, premised as it is 'on the principle of mutual recognition being realized in the new national community, in which the roles of leaders and led are interchangeable'.

This account offers a corrective to those poststructuralist interpretations of nationalism which see it as inescapably hierarchical in both its anti-colonial and post-independence forms, while a notion of anti-colonial political agency based on opposition challenges the critical popularity of negotiation in current criticism. What emerges is that not only these writers but also the political nationalist movements of which they were part need further recognition and positive re-evaluation by contemporary postcolonial studies. This is not simply an historical exercise since, as Cooppan points out, race and nation continue to be invoked in the formation and organisation of post-colonial identities, their significance resisting poststructuralist allegations of essentialism.

Sandhu's essay on the function of metropolitan London in the writing of Hanif Kureishi provides an interpretation which is not reducible to postcolonial theoretical orthodoxies of subject-formation within either the diaspora or the decolonised nation state. Sandhu reads Kureishi's London as a location which facilitates personal liberation for black (as well as white) peoples, but where the relationship between people and city is dialectical: 'its enduring vitality has always been dependent on the willingness of arrivants to use London as an arena for heightened commercial, creative and sexual energy. The sheer momentum and thrill of living in London inspires its peoples to hustle, dream and overcome the limitations that prejudice, penury and timidity create. And, as they do so, London is itself sustained and constituted by their energies'. Through a celebration of London's emancipatory potential, Sandhu maintains, Kureishi produces an oppositional aesthetic, one which 'appropriates' London to the project of cultural democracy, and thereby offers yet another version of subalternity.

Coronil's essay on the contemporary nation state of Venezuela also takes issue with dominant conceptions of 'the subaltern'. Focusing on the brutal repression of mass protests in 1989 against the free-market austerity measures introduced by the new government, Coronil contends that 'subalternity' is a relational and a relative concept since subjects can appear on the social stage both as subaltern actors and as playing dominant roles. By examining the speeches of government representatives during this turbulence, Coronil maintains that by entering into the international terrain of free-market capitalism, the neocolonial state simultaneously assumes a subaltern subject position in the narrative of global capitalism, and an imperial elite subject position which openly harnesses colonial discourse to justify domination over its people, now cast as 'primitive' and 'uncivilised' aliens.

The neocolonial operations of global capitalism, which break down cultural, geographical and economic distinctions between 'metropolis' and 'colony', force a reconceptualisation of state powers and ideologies, and require critics to rethink the relations between 'first world' diasporic subjects and postcolonial subjects resident in formerly colonised nations. Expanding on this last matter, Premnath highlights how postcolonial intellectuals based in the metropolis have used the figure of the migrant 'as the authorizing sign for [his] joint debunking of anti-colonial and imperial nationalism', and contends that 'within the field of postcolonial studies . . . discourses of migrancy and diaspora [have] often worked to disconnect postcolonialist intellectual production from the vicissitudes of the formally independent, formerly-colonised nation-state'.

As a theoretical contribution, the collection as a whole argues against postcolonial conceptualisations derived from static antinomies, and for more dialectical as well as relational approaches. Many of the essays critically interrogate the postcolonial critic Homi Bhabha's keyword 'hybridity' for its inflexibility and partiality. Sandhu posits a notion of cultural identity as formed through 'aggregation' instead of the rigidly dualistic fusion implied by hybridity. For Cooppan hybridity does not replace, but operates alongside, material categories of race and nation. Similarly, in discussing the work of prominent postcolonial critic Gayatri Spivak, Coronil is concerned that the absolutism of her antinomies – which may usefully be reconceptualised as relationships rather than polarised positions – lead her to banish subaltern agency to an unrepresentable space.

If the traditional geographical boundaries of academic postcolonialism are questioned by this collection, so too are its disciplinary borders. The institutionalisation of postcolonial studies within the US academy is critically examined by Cooppan, who recommends its desegregation from English departments and engagement with other analytic pursuits. Other essays suggest the need to understand the dominant theoretical lexicon of contemporary postcolonial studies (Premnath, Sandhu), thereby providing elements of a disciplinary genealogy; while a complementary interest animates Quayson's consideration of the interdisciplinary paradigm for 'a field whose social referent is a peculiarly anguished domain . . . struggling to transcend the effects of colonialism'. A concern with the instrumental value of postcolonial cultural studies for social engagement with the world leads

Quayson to contend that, in a field which has from its inception borrowed from other enquiries and crossed already constituted academic frontiers, 'the interdisciplinary model has ultimately to answer to the ways in which it shapes an ethical attitude to reality, in this case, to postcolonial reality'.

Laura Chrisman and Benita Parry
October 1998

W(h)ither Post-colonial Studies? Towards the Transnational Study of Race and Nation

VILASHINI COOPPAN

I

To MANY OF US who locate our work, with increasing unease, in post-colonial studies, as well as to our colleagues in other fields of literary and cultural analysis, the disciplinary history of post-colonial studies appears one of extraordinary, indeed improbable, rapidity. The accelerated time-line of 'the post-colonial' has served as a point of entry for astute interrogations of the 'pitfalls' of this most current term in contemporary critical discourse.[1] The 'post-colonial' hastily compresses several distinct eras and arenas of colonialism and imperialism,

[1] Anne McClintock, 'The Angel of Progress: Pitfalls of the Term "Post-Colonialism,"' *Social Text* 31/32 (1992), 84–98. McClintock questions in particular 'the orientation of the emerging discipline [of post-colonial studies] and its concomitant theories and curricula changes, around a singular, monolithic term, organized around a binary axis of time rather than power, and which, in its premature celebration of the pastness of colonialism, runs the risk of obscuring the continuities and discontinuities of colonial and imperial power' (88). Other interrogations of the term 'post-colonialism' include: Ella Shohat, 'Notes on the Post-Colonial,' *Social Text* 31/32 (1992), 99–113; Ruth Frankenberg and Lata Mani, 'Crosscurrents, Crosstalk: Race, "Postcoloniality" and the Politics of Location,' *Cultural Studies* 7:2 (1993), 292–310; Laura Chrisman, 'Inventing Post-colonial Theory: Polemical Observations,' *Pretexts* 5:1–2 (1995), 205–12; Stuart Hall, 'When Was the "Postcolonial"? Thinking at the Limit,' *The Post-Colonial Question: Divided Skies, Common Horizons*, ed. Iain Chambers and Linda Curti (New York: Routledge, 1996), 242–60. My hyphenation of 'post-colonial' throughout this essay consciously rejects the popular usage of 'postcolonial' as a term whose unicity effectively erases colonialism as a distinct category with its own continuing effects. The hyphenated term resonates more specifically, invites us to think in more precise historical categories by hearing in 'post-colonial' the echoes of the 'anti' and 'neo' that also precede 'colonial' and that together map out the range of concerns within this discipline. Certainly, there are critics who use the term 'postcolonial' yet remain keenly aware of the historical disjunctures implicit within it. See, for example, Elleke Boehmer, *Colonial and Postcolonial Literature* (New York: Oxford University Press, 1995), especially 8–9.

1

individual struggles of decolonization, subsequent regimes of neo-colonialism and neo-imperialism, and various post-World War II movements of exile, migration, and diaspora into a collective critical entity that effectively homogenizes differences of history and geography, place and politics. Paradoxically, the watchwords of this globalized 'post-coloniality' are heterogeneity, difference, alterity, hybridity. Post-colonial studies, as several of its most incisive critics have noted, has compressed the differences of other people's history on a methodological level while it has simultaneously asserted and celebrated those differences on a theoretical and discursive level.

A similar contradiction governs the ways in which post-colonial studies in the United States academy has approached the narration, which is to say the invention, of its own history as an academic discipline, a field of knowledge, and an institutional presence. On the one hand, the field seems to compress its internal differences in order to lay claim to a single, hitherto empty place in the academy, and an overarching intellectual coherence of the kind that produces 'post-colonial courses,' 'post-colonial criticism,' and 'post-colonialists.' On the other hand, post-colonial studies in its hegemonic US form retains a sense of the differentiated critical methods and agendas housed under its umbrella, but significantly eschews the model of a gathering of difference in favor of a sequential, chronological plotting of the sort that produces the post-colonial reader and the syllabi of post-colonial undergraduate courses that rely on such readers.

In these dominant formations, post-colonial history moves rapidly in a narrative of progress that can be, and frequently is, plotted from the originary moment of Edward Said's 1978 publication of *Orientalism*, through the attempt of colonial discourse analysis to expose within Said's diagnosis of a hegemonizing, overwhelmingly authoritative, imperial will-to-know a more discontented, ambivalent, and fundamentally fractured set of power relations. Part of the impoverishment of this truncated history is its relegation of such responses to Said as the Subaltern Studies group's efforts to locate the heterogenous signs of native presence and local resistance to colonialism, to post-colonial historical scholarship rather than to post-colonial studies per se (which enjoy an alarmingly unidisciplinary literary and literary-critical status in US academic institutions). The end point of this abbreviated disciplinary history seems to be a contemporary mode of reading in which, having been rendered aware of the discursive nature and iterative instability of power, we may proceed to diagnose its textual workings in literary texts rich in the metaphorical tropings not only of certain sharply binarized colonial, anti-colonial, and neo-colonial struggles (Occident vs. Orient, colonizer vs. colonized, metropolitan culture's linguistic and governmental imperium vs. the array of resistant indigenous linguistic, political, cultural, and social practices, a foreign modernity vs. a tradition variously vital or moribund), but also of such blurry markers of 'the post-colonial experience' as national expatriation, linguistic appropriation, cultural syncretism, and identity fragmentation. Lest we rejoice too readily in the emergence of a post-colonial way of reading that is as attuned to ambivalence as to agon, let me note that these two terms are not simultaneously present but rather chronologically plotted – *from* agon *to* ambivalence in dominant versions of post-colonial pedagogy.

Nearly a decade ago, Bill Ashcroft's, Gareth Griffith's, and Helen Tiffin's *The Empire Writes Back* asserted a set of thematic concerns common to all post-colonial literatures, from the creole societies of the Afro-Caribbean to the settler colonies of Canada and Australia. These literatures were seen to share a common textual subversion of imperial polarities, linguistic decentralizing of metropolitan 'English' in favor of a multiplicity of appropriated, reconfigured, liberated 'englishes,' and foregrounding of the 'inevitable,' 'fruitful,' 'syncretic and hybridized nature of post-colonial experience.'[2] More recently and in a US context, Timothy Brennan has diagnosed a widespread 'attack' on dichotomous paradigms in contemporary cultural and post-colonial studies: '[w]e have for some time now been witnessing a shift from a binary otherness to a single, internally rich and disparate plurality . . .'.[3] To use the critical shorthand that unfortunately and too often expresses an entire field of diverse intellectual and political inquiry, we move from the work of Said to that of Homi K. Bhabha, whose anatomy of manifold colonial difference and hybridity, of post-colonial in-between-ness and displacement has become an expected reference in the work of many US critics who write as 'post-colonialists' or, increasingly, in a style visibly marked by post-colonial scholarship.[4] Without dismissing

[2] Bill Ashcroft, Gareth Griffiths, and Helen Tiffin, *The Empire Writes Back: Theory and Practice in Post-Colonial Literatures* (London and New York: Routledge, 1989), chs. 1–3, 30, 41.
[3] Timothy Brennan, *At Home in the World: Cosmopolitanism Now* (Cambridge, Massachusetts, and London: Harvard University Press, 1997), 2.
[4] See the discussion of colonial difference and hybridity in Bhabha's early essays: 'The Other Question – The Stereotype and Colonial Discourse,' *Screen* 24:6 (1983); 'Difference, Discrimination and the Discourse of Colonialism,' in *The Politics of Theory, Proceedings of the Essex Conference on the Sociology of Literature*, ed. Francis Barker (Colchester: University of Essex Press, 1983); 'Of Mimicry

either the paradigm-shifting force of Said's *Orientalism* or the nuance,
intensity, and utility of the debate that emerges from *Orientalism*'s
readers,[5] I would nonetheless question the consequences that this

and Men,' *October* 28 (1984); 'Sly Civility,' *October* 35 (1985); and 'Signs Taken
for Wonders: Questions of Ambivalence and Authority Under a Tree Outside
Delhi,' in '*Race,' Writing, and Difference*, ed. Henry Louis Gates Jr. (London and
Chicago: University of Chicago Press, 1985). Bhabha's seminal essay on the
migrant, in-between nature of post-colonial location is 'DissemiNation: Time,
Narrative, and the Margins of the Modern Nation,' in *Nation and Narration*, ed.
Bhabha (London and New York: Routledge, 1990). Versions of all of these essays
have been usefully collected in *The Location of Culture* (London and New York:
Routledge, 1994). My formulation of a passage 'from Said to Bhabha' is of course
crude, but I wish to draw attention precisely to the reductive nature of dominant
post-colonial critical schemas and to the star system which such schemas
reinforce in the US academy. That said, let me also note that this formulation
glosses over the extent to which Said's work resists association with purely
binarized categories of analysis. See, for example, *Culture and Imperialism* (New
York: Alfred A. Knopf, 1993) which, in addition to exploring the work of a range
of oppositional, anti-colonial intellectuals, also pleads for a recognition of the
fundamental syncretism of cultural formation and culture itself.
[5] Edward Said, *Orientalism* (New York: Vintage, 1978). I am thinking of reviews
of *Orientalism* such as those by James Clifford, *History and Theory* 19:2 (1980),
204–23 and Talal Asad, *English Historical Review* 95 (July 1980), 648–9, as well
as critical explications such as that of Robert Young, *White Mythologies: Writing
History and the West* (London: Routledge, 1990), 119–41. Local elaborations of
Orientalism include Christopher L. Miller's tracing of a parallel discourse of
'Africanism' in *Blank Darkness: Africanist Discourse in French* (Chicago: Uni-
versity of Chicago Press, 1985), Gauri Viswanathan's extrapolation of *Orient-
alism* to the case of British education in India in *Masks of Conquest: Literary
Study and British Rule in India* (New York: Columbia University Press, 1989), and
Lisa Lowe's argument for the 'heterogeneity' of Said's Orientalist object in
Critical Terrains: French and British Orientalism (Ithaca: Cornell University Press,
1991). Critical reconsiderations of *Orientalism* are proffered by Dennis Porter,
'Orientalism and its Problems,' in *The Politics of Theory, Proceedings of the Essex
Conference on the Sociology of Literature*, ed. Frances Barker (Colchester:
University of Essex Press, 1983), 179–1983, Lata Mani and Ruth Frankenberg,
'The Challenge of *Orientalism*,' *Economy and Society* 14:2 (1985), 174–92; and
most polemically, Aijaz Ahmad, *In Theory: Classes, Nations, Literatures*
(London: Verso, 1992), ch. 5. For historically-minded explorations of the
consequence of *Orientalism* for the writing of South Asian histories, see
Orientalism and the Postcolonial Predicament: Perspectives on South Asia, ed.
Carol A. Breckenridge and Peter van der Veer (Philadelphia: University of
Pennsylvania Press, 1993), as well as Sumit Sarkar's critique of 'the Saidian turn
of a section of the Subaltern Studies group' in 'Orientalism Revisited: Saidian
Frameworks in the Writing of Modern Indian History,' *Oxford Literary Review*,
special issue *On India: Writing History, Culture, and Post-Coloniality*, ed. Ania
Loomba and Suvir Kaul, 16:1–2 (1994), 205–24. Finally, excellent discussions

particular narration of disciplinary history has had for post-colonial studies, especially in the United States.

The contestatory work that this article undertakes, namely the mapping of some co-ordinates by which we might locate an alternative disciplinary history and disciplinary practice, is by no means new. Benita Parry has been an especially forceful advocate of an alternative history for post-colonial studies, diagnosing with precision the guiding assumptions and implicit omissions of metropolitan post-colonial theorists such as Said, Spivak, and Bhabha in her article 'Problems in Current Theories of Colonial Discourse' (1987). Elsewhere, Parry has explored post-colonial studies' debts to critical traditions such as the Foucauldian reconceptualization of western power and knowledge as discourse, post-structuralist theories of language, notably Derrida's deconstructive critique of western metaphysics through a sustained engagement with the working of the sign, and the efforts of western Marxism and British cultural studies to theorize the multiple points of articulation that connect base and superstructure, economic and cultural determinations, hegemony and counter-hegemony, subjectivity and agency.[6] It is through such a survey of terminological provenance and theoretical genealogy that we can come to see how selective post-colonial studies has generally been in its borrowings, deploying one particular set of key terms while eliding another. The field's treatment of Fanon stands as an exemplary instance of this discriminating tendency insofar as it foregrounds a Fanon who dramatizes the instability of psychic identification under colonialism's brutalizing rule of racist stereotype and primitivist

---

of *Orientalism* as well as others of Said's works can be found in the essays collected in *Edward Said: A Critical Reader*, ed. Michael Sprinker (Oxford: Blackwell, 1992), and *Reflections on the Work of Edward Said: Secular Criticism and the Gravity of History*, ed. Keith Ansell-Pearson, Benita Parry, and Judith Squires (New York: St. Martins Press, 1997).

[6] Benita Parry, 'Problems in Current Theories of Colonial Discourse,' *Oxford Literary Review*, 9 (1987), 27–58; 'Signs of Our Times,' *Third Text*, 28/29 (1994), 5–24; 'The Postcolonial: Conceptual Category or Chimera?' *The Yearbook of English Studies*, special issue on *The Politics of Postcolonial Criticism*, 27 (1997), 3–21. It is worth noting that the sustained analysis of the contributions of psychoanalysis to post-colonial investigations of power, identity, and resistance has been largely confined to commentaries on Homi Bhabha's work, where psychoanalysis serves as a template, ever in the process of skewing its overlay, for colonial identity. Kalpana Seshadri-Crooks provides an excellent opening into a more historically grounded consideration of the relationship between psychoanalysis and post-coloniality in 'The Primitive as Analyst: Postcolonial Feminism's Access to Psychoanalysis,' *Cultural Critique* 28 (Fall 1994), 175–218.

fantasy over the Fanon whose prophetic accounts of anti-colonial nationalist struggle influenced a world of revolutions.[7] Parry's own injunction to remember Fanon as the promoter of a 'combative subject position' that is oppositionally defined, historically located, and politically revolutionary, and Neil Lazarus's effort to reinscribe the political category of nationalism into an increasingly globalized Fanon suggest an active questioning of dominant post-colonial paradigms common to both sides of the Atlantic.[8] However, the post-colonial scenes into which their respective interrogations emerge are substantially different.

In Britain a strong tradition of cultural studies, rooted in but by no means synonymous with questions of nation and nationalisms, has actively informed a kind of interdisciplinary post-colonial studies that is historicist in method, often materialist in analysis, and explicitly concerned with the connections between discursive regimes, social identities, and political categories, including empire, colony, and anti-colony, nation and globe, local community and diasporic network.[9] In

---

[7] For a comprehensive survey of Fanon's status as a 'global theorist of alterity' in a range of discursive traditions and a valorization of his exilic doubleness as a Martinican turned Algerian, see Henry Louis Gates Jr., 'Critical Fanonism,' *Critical Inquiry* 17 (Spring 1991), 457–70. For a reading of Fanon that argues for his anatomy of colonial racism and racial subjectivity as a dislocating, split-inducing, identity-shattering challenge to Enlightenment ideals of humanity and history, see Bhabha's 'Foreword: Remembering Fanon, Self, Psyche and the Colonial Condition,' in *Black Skin, White Masks*, trans. Charles Lam Markmann (London: Pluto Press, 1986), vii–xxv. Essays that invoke Fanon's originary presence in the discourses of Third World liberation include: Parry, 'Problems' and 'Resistance Theory/Theorising Resistance or Two Cheers for Nativism,' in *Colonial Discourse/Post-Colonial Theory*, ed. Francis Barker and Peter Hulme (Manchester: Manchester University Press, 1994); Cedric J. Robinson, 'The Appropriation of Frantz Fanon,' *Race and Class* 35:1 (July–September 1993), 79–90; Neil Lazarus, 'Disavowing Decolonization: Fanon, Nationalism, and the Problematic of Representation in Current Theories of Colonial Discourse,' *Research in African Literatures* 24:4 (Winter 1993), 69–98.
[8] Parry, 'Problems'; Lazarus, 'Disavowing Decolonization.'
[9] See Peter Hulme, *Colonial Encounters: Europe and the Native Caribbean, 1492–1792* (New York: Routledge, 1992); Bill Schwarz, 'Conquerors of Truth: Reflections on Postcolonial Theory,' in *The Expansion of England: Race, Ethnicity and Cultural History* (London: Routledge, 1996); Annie E.S. Coombes, *Reinventing Africa: Museums, Material Culture and Popular Imagination in Late Victorian and Edwardian England* (New Haven: Yale University Press, 1994); Stuart Hall, 'New Ethnicities,' in *'Race,' Culture and Difference*, ed. James Donald and Ali Rattansi (London: Sage, 1992), 252–49, and 'Cultural Identity and Diaspora,' in *Identity: Community, Culture, Difference*, ed. Jonathan Rutherford (London: Lawrence & Wishart, 1990), 222–37.

the United States, rather more protectionist impulses have held sway, insulating from one another disciplinary inquiries that actually share a common interest in the analysis of changing patterns of domination, subordination, and resistance. The result is a prevailing version of post-colonial studies in the United States that so embraces its aura of 'new work' and its dual allegiances to high theory and a rather reified, distanced, and monolithic 'Third World literature' that it largely estranges itself from the individual and collective histories of several important allied traditions such as American studies, Native American studies, African American studies, Asian American studies, Latino studies, and Gay and Lesbian studies.[10]

In what follows I want to shift the terms in which post-colonial studies in the United States has constructed the story of its origins and refocus attention on two categories, race and nation, that I believe have become dangerously peripheral to what many would see as the 'real' work of the field. The unsavoury histories of these uneasy foundational terms make the process of theoretical partisanship a complex one. To speak for them, it seems, is to advocate a return to a particularly specious kind of essentialist politics. Indeed, to the extent that post-colonial studies in the American academy has reinforced an institutional mindset that certain people are more

---

[10] See Shohat, 'Notes on the Post-Colonial.' For an introduction to some of the possibilities offered by such interdisciplinary alliances, see the following two volumes of essays: *Cultures of United States Imperialism*, ed. Amy Kaplan and Donald E. Pease (Durham: Duke University Press, 1993), especially Kaplan's introductory essay, ' "Left Alone with America": The Absence of Empire in the Study of American Culture' (3–21); and *The Nature and Context of Minority Discourse*, ed. Abdul R. JanMohamed and David Lloyd (New York and London: Oxford University Press, 1990). Specific analyses of post-colonial problematics in the study of ethnic minority experience in the US can be found in: *From Different Shores: Perspectives on Race and Ethnicity in America* (London and New York: Oxford University Press, 1987); Gloria Anzaldua, *Borderlands/La Frontera: The New Mestiza* (San Francisco: Aunt Lute Books Company, 1987); *Criticism in the Borderlands: Studies in Chicano Literature, Culture, and Ideology*, ed. Hector Calderon and José David Saldívar (Durham, NC: Duke University Press, 1991); José David Saldívar, *The Dialectics of Our America: Genealogy, Cultural Critique, and Literary History* (Durham and London: Duke University Press, 1991); and Eva Cherniavsky, 'Subaltern Studies in a U.S. Frame,' *boundary 2* 23:2 (1996), 85–110. Joel Burges has laid out some of the guidelines by which queer theory might 'perver[t] the postcolonial' in ' "The Unnatural History of Civilization": A Ghostly Genealogy of United States Imperialism, Postcolonial Black Nationalism, and Homophobia' (unpublished essay submitted to *The Yale Journal of Criticism*).

appropriate candidates, by virtue of their origin, for the teaching of non-western literatures than others, to advocate for race and nation might be seen to legitimate a grave misreading of the concept of specialization.[11] As disturbing as is the spectre of the analytic categories of race and nation licensing a doctrine of authentic identities, it is also true that without these terms we risk becoming unable to name and investigate some of the most powerful social rifts of recent years, including the conflicts engendered by resurgent ethnic nationalism in the Balkans and Rwanda; the end of apartheid's racial regime of legalized white supremacy and the foundation of a new nation in South Africa; the racist xenophobia that undergirds an emergent pan-European economic and cultural nationalism; and the deep, racialized divides that make the United States something less than 'one nation' at home while securing abroad the continuing profit margins of its most powerful multinational corporations, for whom the Third World serves as global sweatshop.

For my part, I believe that to advocate a return to the terms of race and nation is not to assert their evidentiary, experiential, material, and ultimately fixed status against an effervescent, vaguely post-colonial hybridity. Race and nation are not terms to invoke but terms to investigate, from their histories of purist doctrine from the Enlightenment onwards, to the variegated patterns of their modern cultural constructions and their lived social effects, including their strategic reformulations in the service of oppositional politics. By no means do I mean to suggest that the peculiarly vexed, historically burdened concepts of race and nation should supersede other categories of analysis as the bases of oppositional criticism. Indeed, if post-colonial criticism is to locate race and nation, it can do so only by also marking other axes of social existence. But there is a difference between naming class, gender, and ethnicity as internal differentiations 'implied' within the primary, broadly communitarian terms of race and nation, and theorizing instead the coextensiveness of all these terms, whose specific articulations to one another at distinct historical and political moments constitute the very patterns of systemic domination and organized resistance.

Race and nation, class and ethnicity, gender and sexuality, culture and community, are difficult terms in their local as in their global

[11] Brennan's *Cosmopolitanism Now* takes on the difficult task of naming this particular institutional phenomenon and the related debates in the US academy around affirmative action, especially on 114–18.

formations. Referring both to analytic categories and to constructed constituencies, these are terms within which individuals are not simply 'represented' but themselves engage in complex processes of identification and contestation. Often we must learn to read these terms with regard both to their conjunctions with one another and their internal disjunctions, for example the dissonance between the invocation of nation and the ethnicized, racialized, gendered, and classed subjects who inhabit its geographical and social peripheries (refugees, migrants, immigrants, the undocumented, 'guest workers').[12] We must also remain able to distinguish between oppositional uses of these concepts, and those which further absolutist politics.[13]

Given the complexity and undeniability of these conceptual crossings, why do my remarks here focus so insistently on race and nation, seemingly at the expense of the various modalities in which they are expressed and of the various analytical categories with which they are entwined? Because no critical project speaks independent from or outside of its history, it is perhaps wise to proceed no farther without an account of the genesis that this essay represents.

From where I write, one burden of this project is the critical

[12] See in this regard Immanuel Wallerstein's distinction between classes ('objective analytical categories') and nations, races, and ethnic groups, all of which refer to constructed 'peoples' who correlate to certain classes. In Wallerstein's indexing of these latter categories to structural features of the capitalist world economy, nation refers to a historical system of hierarchically structured, mutually competitive sovereign states, race names the disparity between core and periphery and the stratification of work across the international division of labor, and ethnicity refers to a system of stratified occupations within the state. Wallerstein's rather divisive mapping of racialization in transnational contexts and ethnicization within national and state boundaries can be usefully compared with Arjun Appadurai's account of the ways in which ethnicity and culture come to be constructed and figured in explicitly transnational and diasporic ways. Wallerstein in Wallerstein and Etienne Balibar, *Race, Nation and Class: Ambiguous Identities* (New York: Verso, 1991), trans. Chris Turner (of Balibar), 79–83; Appadurai, 'Disjuncture and Difference in the Global Cultural Economy,' *Public Culture* 2:2 (Spring 1990), 1–24; *Modernity at Large: Cultural Dimensions of Globalization* (Minneapolis: University of Minnesota Press, 1996).

[13] For a negotiation of this tension see Stuart Hall's discussion of the 'hybridization' and 'diaspora-ization' of nation and culture and the concomitant dangers of 'forms of national and cultural identity – new or old – which attempt to secure *their* identity by adopting closed versions of culture or community . . .,' 'Culture, Community, Nation,' *Cultural Studies* 7:3 (1993), 349–63, 361, as well as the critical exchange between Saba Mahmood and Hall in 10:1 (1996), 1–15.

interrogation of the role that post-colonial studies has played in the American academy, where it has been largely institutionalized under the auspices of departments of English literature and where it has had surprisingly few formal alliances with other fields of oppositional criticism, for example, the various ethnic studies programs, the historical study of race and racism, the transnational analysis of global capitalisms and global cultures. Such a placing of the field within the American academy bypasses, for example, the question of whether the existence of what some have called a 'domestic Third World' comprised of those marginalized on the basis of race, ethnicity, gender, class, citizenship, and language use, can be plotted into colonial schemas and with what effects.[14] The Americanized version of post-colonial studies also places its practitioners at an untenable, for many of us unthinkable, distance from the other parts of the world to which this field of inquiry has traveled or, less euphemistically, been exported. Consider, for example, questions that South Africa poses to post-colonial paradigms in light of that country's creation under apartheid of

---

[14] Some US academics charge that we should hesitate to equate the processes of marginalization at work within the United States with some kind of 'domestic Third World' because the latter term homogenizes too readily the internal differences among minority communities in the United States and the larger differences between the United States and non-metropolitan countries. In *Racial Formation in the United States* (1986, New York: Routledge, 1994), Michael Omi and Howard Winant caution against the 'internal colonialism' thesis of the 1960s and 1970s that held minority communities to be subject to colonial forms of control including spatial division along racial lines, cultural domination, exploitation, and externalization of the institutions of power (44–6). See, for example, Kwame Ture (Stokely Carmichael) and Charles V. Hamilton, *Black Power: The Politics of Liberation in America* (1968, New York: Vintage, 1992), chs. 1–3 and Robert Blauner, *Racial Oppression in America* (New York: Harper and Row, 1972). For Omi and Winant the internal colonialism thesis and its attendant cultural nationalism cannot account for divisions of class within minority communities, interminority group rivalries, or the interpenetration of minority and dominant cultures; because colonial paradigms 'reason by analogy, they cannot range over the uniqueness and complexities of American racial ideology or politics' (162, fn. 4). In 'Crosscurrents, Crosstalk: Race, "Postcoloniality," and the Politics of Location' Lata Mani and Ruth Frankenberg argue against the adequacy of the term "postcolonial" in a US context. They instead propose the term 'post-Civil Rights,' acutely aware of the term's ironic resonances in evoking both the completion of a historic era of ethnic-based social movements and the radically unfinished nature of that project in the contemporary US.

a form of internal racialized subordination popularly termed in intellectual and political critique 'colonialism of a special type,' followed by its 1994 transition to a free, democratic, 'non-racial state' and, to borrow Nicholas Visser's cleverly coined term, 'post-colonialism of a special type.'[15] If my exploration of these questions here has something of the autobiographical to it insofar as it focuses primarily on the status of post-colonial studies within the American academy, where I live and teach, while also referencing the contested intersections between post-colonial paradigms and the 'new South Africa,' where I have also taught and where I claim my citizenship, I trust that it will also be something more than a personal placing.

II

Over the past twenty years of its self-proclaimed history post-colonial studies, especially in the United States, has been fortunate to have been subjected to criticisms of the most exacting order, which have pushed it in such necessary directions as the interrogation and resignification of its terms (the 'post-colonial' foremost among these), the theorization of the metropolitan privilege that post-colonial theory and theorists enjoy by virtue of their location within the Euro-American academy, and the consideration of the political consequences of the field's rapid rise to academic power. It has become standard for progressive-minded critics of the academic institution of post-colonial studies to highlight the disjunction between the field's eponymous announcement of the passing of colonialism and imperialism and the continuing neo-colonialist and neo-imperialist dominance of formally independent nations by the powerful alliance of Euro-American nationalism and transnational capital.[16] Equally deserving of

---

[15] Nicholas Visser, 'Postcoloniality of a Special Type: Theory and Its Appropriations in South Africa,' *Yearbook of English Studies* 27 (1997), 79–94.

[16] See the essays by McClintock and Shohat in the special issue of *Social Text* dedicated to interrogations of post-colonialism [31/32 (1992)]; Frankenberg and Mani, 'Crosscurrents, Crosstalk'; Masao Miyoshi, 'A Borderless World? From Colonialism to Transnationalism and the Decline of the Nation-State,' *Critical Inquiry* 19:4 (Summer 1993), 726–51; Chrisman, 'Inventing Postcolonial Theory'; Hall, 'When Was the "Postcolonial"?'; Aijaz Ahmad, 'The Politics of Literary Post-coloniality,' *Race and Class* 36:3 (1995), 1–20; McClintock, *Imperial Leather: Race, Gender and Sexuality in the Colonial Contest* (New York: Routledge, 1995), 1–17, 391–6; and the essays collected in *Dangerous Liaisons: Gender, Nation, and Postcolonial Perspectives* (Minneapolis:

attention is the divide and conquer phenomenon observed by Ella Shohat, namely that 'the post-colonial' often serves as a more palatable, more readily assimilable, 'pastoral' version of difference to academic institutions than 'any language invoking issues such as "imperialism and third worldist critique," "neo-colonialism and resisting cultural practices," and "the geopolitics of cultural exchange." '[17]

There is another disjunction, visible on a terminological level, which I will schematize in terms of an opposition between the analytic concept of hybridity and the categories of race and nation.[18] As Shohat notes, the rapid popularity of 'the post-colonial' has displaced other fields of oppositional inquiry, many of them with extensive histories of their own. Yet a dissenting point of view might argue that 'the post-colonial' is not a single, invading monolith but rather encompasses a wide range of critical practices and theoretical affiliations. There are many 'post-colonialisms' contending within the signifier of 'the post-colonial' and it is in fact this mobility of reference that secures for 'the post-colonial' an oppositional status that is none other than the indeterminacy and elusiveness of the sign itself. The difficulty with this logic for me lies in the fact that, among the multiple and proliferating significations of 'the post-colonial,' some have been more equal than others. The post-colonial studies that speak in the language of discursive analysis and through such concepts as hybridity, cultural fusion, and cross-ethnic, transnational intermixture have been subject to substantially greater academic reproduction than those which speak, and indeed have spoken for over a century now, in the languages of materialist analysis, of strategic political identification, of armed resistance and through such concepts as race and nation.[19]

University of Minnesota Press, 1997), eds. McClintock, Shohat, and Aamir Mufti.

[17] Ella Shohat, 'Notes on the "Post-Colonial"', 99.

[18] This distinction, while it is indebted to and bears similarities to Ahmad's delineation in 'The Politics of Literary Post-coloniality' of 'identitarian-particularist' and 'globalising-hybridist' strands in contemporary cultural theory (18), also seeks to explore the traffic between these terms, as well as the conceptual limitations of such terms themselves.

[19] See Parry, 'Problems,' and 'Signs of the Times'; Ahmad, 'The Politics of Literary Post-coloniality'; Arif Dirlik, 'The Postcolonial Aura: Third World Criticism in the Age of Global Capitalism,' *Critical Inquiry* 20:2 (1994), 328–56; Kelwyn Sole, 'South Africa Passes the Posts,' *Alternation, Journal of the Centre for the Study of Southern African Literature and Languages* 4:1 (1997), 116–51.

Insofar as post-colonial studies have privileged theories of hybridity, syncretism, and intermixture as ways to make sense of contemporary political and cultural reality, they have done so through largely textual models. In fact, the presence of hybridity as a thematic concern (colonial native mimics and 'in-between' diasporic migrants) and/or a literary device (the appropriation and reworking of classical western genres, fables, narratives) issues for some critics a kind of guarantee that the text in question is in fact properly 'post-colonial.'[20] Salman Rushdie's *The Satanic Verses* (1989) and Tayeb Salih's *Season of Migration to the North* (1969) offer canonical illustrations; David Dabydeen's semi-autobiographical 1984 novel *The Intended* provides another such example. Its portrait of the hybridity of post-imperial cultures is both powerful and poignant, interweaving the lives of a group of black British schoolboys ('the regrouping of the Asian diaspora in a South London schoolground,') with richly textured recollections of the cultural and ethnic mix of the narrator's Guyanese childhood.[21] The novel is one in which culture eventually wins out, wreaking its syncretic justice on the former seat of metropolitan power and its purist ideologies. The narrator reads his way into Cambridge, subjecting his friends to lengthy disquisitions on the theme of 'suffering and redemption' (97) in Conrad's *Heart of Darkness*. Meanwhile, his Rastafarian friend Joseph steals a video camera and begins to create 'a different kind of book' (105), first a film version of *Heart of Darkness*, then an ambitious project for an allegorical treatment of immigrant experience in a racist Britain, 'a complete statement of the condition of England' (156). Joseph commits suicide before either film sees completion, and it falls to another of the boys to sum up the state of the post-imperial nation. Patel, a Gujerati Hindu who has found financial success in pimping his white girlfriend, announces in the novel's penultimate paragraph: 'All they [the white English] have over us is money . . . and any monkey can make money, once you learn the trick. Soon we'll have more than them, and England will be one tribe of Patels. English people will have names like Lucinda Patel and Egbert Smythe-Patel, wait and see boy' (245–6).

In its depiction of a hybridity that operates in the realms of culture, art, and even, in Patel's prophecy, biology, *The Intended* manages to capture both the transculturative effects of the post-colonial migrations to former metropolitan seats of empire, and the bitter smallness of these

---

[20] See Ashcroft, Slemon, and Tiffin, *The Empire Writes Back*.
[21] David Dabydeen, *The Intended* (London: Secker & Warburg, 1991), 5.

triumphs in a society that remains harshly stratified. Here hybridity does not so much do away with race and nation as provide them with new registers of expression. A critical reading of Dabydeen's novel that would assimilate it into the realm of post-colonial writing largely on the basis of its thematic and stylistic concerns with syncretism threatens to miss the complexity with which the novel articulates the promise of hybridity and the visceral pathos of ethnic nationalism and racialist thinking – an articulation whose modulations, both gross and fine, we cannot afford to ignore if we are to understand post-coloniality in any serious way.

With scrupulous attention to the importance of the category of 'nation' in contemporary literary, cultural, and political analysis, Tim Brennan has contextualized the current popularity of the term 'hybridity' within a larger discourse of cosmopolitanism and specifically within the 'cosmopolitan drift of colonial theory.'[22] In his outline of the distinct senses among which the term 'hybridity' easily slides, Brennan usefully identifies the following: 'a confessional meaning, involving an account of the consequences of being foreign by race or upbringing, and yet well positioned, influential, respected in certain circles precisely for one's foreignness'; a reference 'poignantly to the mixed origins of a metropolitan culture that, in spite of these mixings, is consistently portrayed as stable'; and a 'political strategy of negotiation or compromise under the current system – the familiar "war of position" taken inaccurately out of Gramsci and made to serve a theoretical stance that exaggerates the politically strategic role of culture itself' (13–14). In addition to the highly influential work of Homi Bhabha on hybridity (to whom, among others, Brennan is responding) I am also thinking, in my remarks on the ease with which hybridity displaces race and nation, of the very differently located projects of Kwame Anthony Appiah's *In My Father's House* and Paul Gilroy's *The Black Atlantic*. These two texts strenuously question the relevance of nation- and race-based thinking in the contexts of contemporary Africa (Appiah) and the transnational triangle of the Afro-Caribbean, Black Britain, and Black America

---

[22] Brennan, *At Home in the World*, 58. Ahmad also criticizes the notion, popularized by Rushdie and Bhabha, of an intercultural hybridity crystallized in the figure of the cosmopolitan migrant for its dismissal of imperialist capital's global penetration, of the proliferation of ethnic enclaves and the consolidation of the nation-state form, of the 'inequal relations of cultural power *today*,' and of the conditions for socialist change ('The Politics of Literary Post-coloniality,' 16–17).

(Gilroy), both of which are seen to be more profoundly and powerfully marked by such phenomena as the diversity of ethnic communities, the processes of cultural contact and transculturation, and the syncretic force of culture itself. Thus Appiah charges, '[t]he truth is that there are no races; there is nothing in the world that can do all we ask race to do for us,' and bids us to consign the term and its biologizing of culture to the historical dustbin.[23] Gilroy, too, invokes the language of obsolescence in defining the Black Atlantic as a 'modern political and cultural formation' that 'can be defined, on one level, through this desire to transcend both the structures of the nation-state and the constraints of ethnicity and national particularity.'[24]

It is difficult to reconcile the image of a post-colonial world in which hybrid identities have triumphed over such narrow particularisms as race and ethnicity, class and gender, nation and nationalism, with the events of the past decade within and outside the United States, beginning in full neo-imperialist mode with the 1991 Gulf War and continuing through such international policies as the forcible repatriation under Bush and then Clinton of Haitian refugees fleeing a murderous regime, and such domestic events as the growing state initiatives to deny gay and lesbian civil rights, to restrict immigration, to mandate 'English-only' education, and to dismantle affirmative action. Even the global optimism over South Africa's transition from apartheid rule to a free, democratic, and non-racial state (Africa's 'dream' to Rwanda's 'nightmare' of ethnic warfare, writes the Nigerian novelist and playwright Wole Soyinka, quoted approvingly in *The New York Times*[25]) cannot ignore the continuing legacies of racialized inequality nor the persistent appeals to ethnic and racial identification by current political parties.[26]

[23] Kwame Anthony Appiah, *In My Father's House: Africa in the Philosophy of Culture* (New York and Oxford: Oxford University Press, 1992), 45.

[24] Paul Gilroy, *The Black Atlantic: Modernity and Double Consciousness* (Cambridge: Harvard University Press, 1993), 19. For critiques of Gilroy's readiness to imagine the transcendence of precisely these modes of affiliation and their historical and present service in oppositional politics, see the following reviews of *The Black Atlantic*: Neil Lazarus, 'Is a Counterculture of Modernity a Theory of Modernity?' *Diaspora* 4:3 (1995), 323–40; Laura Chrisman, 'Journeying to Death: Gilroy's *Black Atlantic*,' *Race and Class* 29:2 (1997), 51–64.

[25] R.W. Apple Jr., 'Into Africa: Just by Going, Clinton Shows Africans U.S. Wants to Keep Their Hopes Up,' *The New York Times* (March 24, 1998).

[26] Among political events of the past four years, consider the Inkatha Freedom Party's expansion of its base beyond those identified with Zulu nationalism to include a range of ethnic/ethnicist communities; the white Afrikaner Freedom

The particularisms of identity are far from disappearing; indeed, they seem to emerge with especial force precisely now when, by all accounts, a brave new world has displaced old affiliative categories and disseminated instead a profusion of decentered and hybridized identities. The very temporal proximity, even simultaneity, of post-colonial pathos and post-colonial promise (Rwanda's 'nightmare' to South Africa's 'dream') seems to have produced a narrative of chronological disjuncture, from the disillusion of narrow identitarianism to the emancipatory optimism of cultural mixture, that approaches the fetishistic logic of disavowal. Knowing how much of the contemporary politics of formerly colonized parts of the world remain imaginatively and otherwise bound to the constructs of race, nation, and class, yet asserting *quand même* the dissolution of those constructs and the emerging reign of an ever more diffuse, multiple, and heterogenous 'culture,' post-colonial political, cultural, and literary discourse falls prey to the progressivist impulses of its vision of history. Texts that fall within the category of 'post-colonial' are not only those which fictionally thematize cultural contact and the absurdities, impurities, and syncretisms that it produces, but also those which represent, in a variety of genres including the novel, the oral poem, the manifesto, the essay, and the *communiqué*, particular (and often particularist) anti-colonial, anti-imperial, and anti-capitalist energies, practices, politics, and polemics. It is crucial that we include the latter in our emerging canons rather than simply relegate them to the prehistory of the post-colonial. To argue that one of these two sets of texts is more properly post-colonial than the other does not get us very far. In a sense, the field of post-colonial studies itself loses in this terminological conflict, whose effect has been to polarize categories that are more properly understood as imbricated with one another – agon and ambivalence, discursive and materialist, textual and social, imaginative fiction and political non-fiction, hybrid and particular.

Front's campaign for a separate white *Volkstaat*; and the formerly ruling National Party's efforts to disavow its apartheid roots and bring so-called Coloureds, Indians, and Africans within its embrace on the basis of an overt platform of common interest and non-racialism and a covert appeal to reject black affiliations. Sociologist Heribert Adam has very recently suggested that official discourse, 'a romanticised "rainbowism" of merging colours is contradicted by the reality of heightened ethno-racial consciousness' ['Real Patriotism, Not Shosholoza,' *Siyaya!* 1:2 (Winter 1998), 12–14]. The emergence of a new parliamentary Commission for the Promotion and Protection of the Rights of Cultural, Religious and Linguistic Communities has also showcased the national debate on ethnicity and race.

Ania Loomba, commenting on Benita Parry and Abdul JanMohamed's advocacy of an antagonistically lived, starkly dichotomized divide between colonized and colonized as an alternative to what they see as Bhabha's evacuation of subaltern agency through a model of colonial hybridity grounded in the enunciative instability of textual pronouncements, terms the opposition a 'not particularly fertile' one. While rigorous in her own critique of Bhabha's 'problematic shift' from 'a particular act of enunciation to a theory of all utterance' and of that shift's corollary whereby the 'hybridity of enunciation spills over into becoming the definitive characteristic of *all* colonial authority, everywhere, at any time,' Loomba nonetheless cautions that '[i]t is difficult to accept that any notion of hybridity will dilute the violence of the colonial encounter,' especially given the 'variegat[ed]' nature of a colonial rule, for example in British India, that did not obliterate indigenous culture, traditions, and forms of governance but rather was forced to contend with and absorb them in order to consolidate its own subordinating efficacy.[27] Loomba's further elaboration of a hybridity that is 'different' from that which Parry and Jan Mohamed criticize and from that which Bhabha glosses, insofar as it challenges critical monopolies on individual terms, effectively opens up within postcolonial critical discourse a lever with which to move it. Rather than accept the dichotomous mapping of post-colonialism's field of discourse into those who celebrate hybridity and those who eschew it in favor of more essentializable (which is not to say essentialized) categories of identity, Loomba's theoretical move importantly emphasizes that there are varieties of the hybrid, some of which operate by means of the very terms that the hybrid is thought to banish, for example caste and class, tribe and ethnicity, race and nation.

Although race and nation seem to have fallen along the historical wayside of post-colonial studies, these constructs and the broader political and cultural discourses they instantiate continue to be very much with us. While on the one hand, the rise of transnational corporatism has realigned economic control outside the boundaries of individual nation-states and thereby brought into question the viability of national models for the analysis of global capitalism,[28] the

---

[27] Ania Loomba, 'Overworlding the "Third World",' *Oxford Literary Review* 13 (1991), special issue, *Neo-colonialism*, 164–91, 172–3. Loomba refers to Parry, 'Problems,' Bhabha, 'Signs Taken for Wonders,' and JanMohamed, 'The Economy of Manichean Allegory: The Function of Racial Difference in Colonialist Literature,' in *'Race,' Writing and Difference*, 78–106.

[28] See Miyoshi, 'A Borderless World.'

distribution of transnational profits retains a distinctly familiar flow reminiscent of an earlier era of imperialist nationalism; labor and consumption circle the globe while wealth, unsurprisingly, does not. Within individual nation-states, the processes of inequitable distribution and their linkages to patterns of racialization and class stratification are urgently contemporary concerns. With regard to race, academic discourse on race may foreground its relatively 'new' status as cultural construction, but advocates of a bio-genetic model of the reproduction of racial inequality remain. Others on the frontlines of conservative cultural politics in the United States are quick to proclaim what Dinesh D'Souza calls 'The End of Racism,' which somehow always seems to entail the end of race altogether.[29] Progressive critics attune to the 'necessary polymorphism of racism' describe the emergence of a new 'racism without races' that happily admits the cultural-differentialist rather than biological-inegalitarian parameters of the term 'race' without, however, changing its inscription in a fundamentally hierarchizing world view.[30]

As Paul Gilroy notes, in contemporary Britain 'no mention is made of old-style biological races at all' but the machinery of racialization works on, finding in an ever more 'reductively conceived' culture the grounds for pathologized differentiation: dissolute and lazy Afro-Caribbeans, backwardly traditional and hard-working Asians.[31] The use of the term 'race' within such projects does not delimit a particular theory of social being, still less an ontological essence, but rather what David Theo Goldberg terms a 'fluid and fragile' *conception*, embedded within historical processes, social identifications, and cultural formations, 'transformed and historically transforming.'[32] Michael Omi and Howard Winant, ethnic studies

[29] Charles Murray and Richard J. Herrnstein, *The Bell Curve: Intelligence and Class Structure in American Life* (Free Press, 1994); Dinesh D'Souza, *The End of Racism: Principles for a Multiracial Society* (Free Press, 1995).
[30] Etienne Balibar, 'Racism and Nationalism,' and 'Is there a Neo-racism?' in Balibar and Wallerstein, *Race, Nation and Class*, 36–67, 48 and 17–28.
[31] Paul Gilroy, 'One Nation Under a Groove,' 'The Peculiarities of the Black English,' and 'Nationalism, History and Ethnic Absolutism,' in *Small Acts: Thoughts on the Politics of Black Cultures* (London and New York: Serpent's Tail, 1993), 19–48, 49–62, 63–73, especially 56–7, 63–5. Also see Hall, 'New Ethnicities'; Henry A. Giroux, 'Living Dangerously: Identity Politics and the New Cultural Racism: Towards a Critical Pedagogy of Representation,' *Cultural Studies* 7:2 (1993), 1–27.
[32] David Theo Goldberg, *Racist Culture: Philosophy and the Politics of Meaning* (Oxford: Blackwell, 1993), 80–1.

scholars who have argued strongly for the continuing relevance of race as a category in US social and political analysis, suggest that we think of race as 'an unstable and "decentered" complex of social meanings constantly being transformed by political struggle' and of racial formation as 'the sociohistorical process by which racial categories are created, inhabited, transformed, and destroyed.'[33] To locate race within post-colonial studies is not to argue for its adoption as a transhistorical universal, a static critical paradigm for how to think about an equally fixed 'identity.' In fact, race must be placed within post-colonial frameworks of analysis not once but many times and in multiple ways. A post-colonial studies unable to theorize the changing forms and local contexts of the category of race, or its insertion within historically distinct changing forms and local con-texts, its insertion within historically distinct processes of racializa-tion, ethnicization, and class stratification, its articulation to other categories of social and psychic identity, and its labile new deploy-ments across the ideological spectrum, is a discipline alienated from at least some of the circumstances of its world.

III

It is perhaps through the reintroduction of the categories of race and nation that post-colonial studies can begin to articulate a different history for its major concepts and for itself. This gesture is not meant to replace the hybridity that has become synonymous with the post-colonial with an equally formulaic invocation of race and nation, but rather to investigate the imbrications of all three terms in a context that is both comparative and historical. Some of the coordinates of such scholarship can be derived from work in fields not popularly considered part of post-colonial studies, for example, the study of slavery. Historians of slavery have for some time emphasized the importance of transnational analyses of slaving societies, slave cultures, and the tri-continental network of the slave trade itself, but literary scholars of slavery are still laying the groundwork for comparative work on the genres, narratives, and representational codes unleashed by the

[33] Omi and Winant, *Racial Formation in the United States*, 55. Also see Winant, 'Difference and Inequality: Postmodern Racial Politics in the US,' in *Racism, the City and the State*, ed. Malcolm Cross and Michael Keith (New York: Routledge, 1993), 108–27.

trauma of slavery and the histories of rebellion.[34] From Aphra Behn's
Oroonoko (1688), whose eponymous hero is a cosmopolitan African
prince fluent in English, French, and Spanish and graced with 'Roman'
features and European sensibilities, to the loving evocations of a slave
culture that has woven itself into the very fabric of American society in
W.E.B. Du Bois's *The Souls of Black Folk* (1903), the Black slave has
been a sentimentalized yet powerful locus of cultural collision and
cultural syncretism. There is a compelling genealogy for post-colonial
studies to unearth from the slave narratives of the self-proclaimed
'black Englishman' Olaudah Equiano (1789) and the future African-
American statesman Frederick Douglass (1845), both of which locate
the Black slave as at once the despised racial other of a dominant
nation and as the finest representative of that nation's ruling ideologies
(British mercantilist capitalism and missionary Christianity for
Equiano, American revolutionary democracy for Douglass).[35]

[34] Among the vast historical literature on slavery, excellent introductions to the
agendas of comparative analysis can be found in: David Brion Davis, *The Problem
of Slavery in Western Culture* (London and New York: Oxford University Press,
1988) and *Slavery and Human Progress* (London and New York: Oxford
University Press, 1984); Robin Blackburn, *The Overthrow of Colonial Slavery
1776–1848* (London: Verso, 1989) and *Making of New World Slavery: From the
Baroque to the Modern, 1492–1800* (London: Verso, 1998); and, in a more
philosophical vein, Orlando Patterson's *Slavery and Social Death: A Comparative
Study* (Cambridge, MA: Harvard University Press, 1985). There is an equally
broad and well-known tradition of scholarship on the literature of slavery,
particularly the slave narratives written or dictated by some six thousand fugitive
or manumitted African American slaves. Introductions to this body of work can
be found in: *The Art of Slave Narrative: Original Essays in Criticism and Theory*, ed.
John Sekora and Darwin T. Turner (Macomb, IL: Western Illinois University
Press, 1982); *The Slave's Narrative*, ed. Charles H. Davis and Henry Louis Gates
Jr. (New York: Oxford University Press, 1985); Frances Foster Smith, *Witnessing
Slavery: The Development of Ante-Bellum Slave Narratives* (Westport: Greenwood
Press, 1979); Robert B. Stepto, *From Behind the Veil: A Study of Afro-American
Narrative* (Urbana: University of Illinois Press, 1979). Gilroy's *The Black Atlantic*
contains an influential discussion of slavery within the contexts of transnational
cultural analysis, and will no doubt lead to more literary studies that seek to
integrate the analysis of African American slave writing and writing about
slavery with inquiry into other national traditions. William Luis's *Voices from
Under: Black Narrative in Latin America and the Caribbean* (Westport, CT:
Greenwood Press, 1984) has importantly introduced English-speaking readers
to a more broadly hemispheric survey of the literary tradition of slavery, while
Moira Ferguson has exhaustively investigated the representation of slavery in
eighteenth-century England in *Subject to Others: British Women Writers and
Colonial Slavery, 1670–1834* (New York: Routledge, 1992).
[35] See Houston A. Baker's discussion of Equiano's and Douglass's narratives in

Equiano, a West African slave on British vessels trading in the West Indies and the Atlantic seaboard, decides himself to 'commence merchant,' and through a series of canny transactions in glass tumblers, Geneva spirits, fruits, and meat, turns his initial threepence into funds sufficient to buy first a Bible and eventually his own freedom – a freedom whose ironies are visible in his manumitted status as paid sailor and chief purchaser of new slaves.[36] Equiano's ascension to merchant-hood prefigures, in the religious conversion plot so characteristic of early slave narratives, his subsequent rise into the far-reaching realms both of Christian evangelicism and imperial trade. The narrative closes with a reproduction of a petition presented by Equiano to the queen 'on behalf of my African brethren' in which he argues for abolition on the basis that it will be good for British trade: 'I doubt not, if a system of commerce was established in Africa, the demand for manufactures will most rapidly augment, as the native inhabitants will insensibly adopt the British fashions, manners, customs &c. In proportion to the civilization, so will be the consumption of British manufactures' (175–6). Equiano targets, indeed himself seems to occupy, the national self-interest of Britain. This sliding between racial and national identities, between the confines of slavery and the expanses of British mercantilism, leads some critics to characterise Equiano as a 'genuine intermediary' and his *Narrative* as one dominated by acciculturative energies, while it causes others to interpret his shifting point of view and changing allegiances as a function of a 'bifurcated self-imaging' that itself mirrors a radically split world.[37] Either, or perhaps both syncretic and schizophrenic, Equiano's call for Britain to exploit not the flesh of Africans but rather the natural resources of the continent and the imitative tendencies and social desires of its inhabitants essentially replaces one order of commodity fetishism (slavery) with another (colonial mercantile capitalism). Equiano's rhetorical gesture,

the first chapter of *Blues, Ideology, and Afro-American Literature* (Chicago and London: The University of Chicago Press, 1984). Eric Sundquist examines Douglass's 'seizure of American rights' in *To Wake the Nations: Race in the Making of American Literature* (Cambridge, MA: Harvard University Press, 1993).

[36] *The Interesting Narrative of the Life of Olaudah Equiano or Gustavus Vassa, the African, The Classic Slave Narratives*, ed. Henry Louis Gates Jr. (New York: Mentor/Penguin, 1987), 1–182, 84.

[37] See respectively, William L. Andrews, 'The First Fifty Years of the Slave Narrative, 1760–1810,' in *The Art of the Slave Narrative*, 1–22, 19; Chinosole, 'Tryin' to Get Over: Narrative Posture in Equiano's Autobiography,' in *The Art of the Slave Narrative*, 45–54, 51.

while it operates on the basis that slavery and empire constitute alternatives to one another, cannot help but reveal beneath the fiction of an obverse relation the coordinates of a deeply intimate crossing, one which post-colonial studies has explored far too little.[38]

Half a century after Equiano's narrative, Frederick Douglass's *Narrative* again explores the complex positioning process by which the Black slave speaks not simply in criticism of the nation but, in some fundamental sense, *as* the nation, through its most privileged discourses and by means of its most charged symbols. Along with the famous moment of resistance when the slave Douglass wrests his master to the ground and that when he escapes by means of a pass he has himself written, stands the dramatic instance when Douglass places himself outside the status of slave not by the triumphalist occupation of the taboo realms of autonomous physical action or literacy but rather by an interrogation of democracy itself. Describing slave life on his former master's plantation for the benefit of his abolitionist audience, Douglass wryly observes: 'A representative could not be prouder of his election to a seat in the American Congress, than a slave on one of the out-farms would be of his election to do errands at the Great House Farm.'[39] The analogy of slave and Congressional representative performs a humanizing function, insisting as it does both that slaves are men and that some party politicians are slaves. The secondary comparison of slave plantation and Congress enacts a criticism, fracturing the meaning and purchase of representational democracy by rendering hollow one of its most potent signs. In Douglass's argument, democracy does not exist because slavery does. It is therefore those who speak against slavery who speak most truly in the tradition of revolutionary democracy.

Equiano's and Douglass's appropriations of the highly resonant national idioms of mercantilism, Christianity, and democracy in the interests of expressing racial identity and racial liberation at once imbricate the realms of national and racial signification and find in their interplay a powerful figure for the hybridity of slavery. When persons considered as commodities aspire to the status of merchant and

---

[38] Some of the possibilities of such investigation, explored from within the context of American studies but relevant nonetheless to post-colonial studies, are addressed by Marion Rust in 'The Subaltern as Imperialist: Speaking of Olaudah Equiano,' in *Passing and the Fictions of Identity*, ed. Elaine K. Ginsberg (Durham and London: Duke University Press, 1996), 21–36.

[39] *Narrative of the Life of Frederick Douglass*, *The Classic Slave Narratives*, 243–331, 262.

citizen, the process of becoming a subject becomes intimately linked with that of incorporating or imitating difference, becoming a self in part through becoming the other. This dynamic, so powerful a thematic in the representation of slavery and freedom, is also a guiding, frequently an overwhelming, concern of hegemonic post-colonial theory. This latter body of scholarship, I am suggesting, is informed to a far greater degree than it has yet acknowledged by narratives of hybridity beyond those of 'the mimic men' of colonialism (the phrase is V.S. Naipaul's in his 1967 novel of the same name) and what Hanif Kureishi's film My Beautiful Laundrette calls the 'in-betweens' created by the post-colonial Asian diaspora in England. Among the other narratives of hybridity to which we might profitably turn our attention are the stories of racial domination and racial liberation, including slavery and abolition but also colonialism, imperialism, and their variegated forms of resistance.

From Negritude on, anti-colonial movements seized and rearticulated for their own ends such dominant discourses of western identity as humanism, psychoanalysis, racial and national consciousness, and a modernizing 'progress.' Fanon's Black Skin, White Masks and The Wretched of the Earth have become post-colonial studies' privileged illustrations of the sustained engagement with, and profound transformation of, these narratives of European identity. Fanon, meanwhile, has become something along the lines of a disciplinary patron saint. Through the analysis of Fanon and often, as both Henry Louis Gates, Jr. and Cedric J. Robinson have noted, through the 'appropriation' of Fanon for various theoretical agendas, post-colonial studies has elaborated many of its most urgent questions including the nature and locales of resistance, the formation of subaltern identities, and the fate of national culture and post-colonial independence. With regard to the specific analysis of race and nation, Fanon presents post-colonial studies with an oeuvre whose explicit agenda is to move beyond the prisonhouse of race and racial thinking to the liberatory space of universalist humanism (in Black Skin, White Masks) and of the decolonized nation (in The Wretched of the Earth and Fanon's other writings on the Algerian revolution). This attempt to identify transracially and transnationally, culminating in the FLN's eulogy for this black Martinican whom they hailed as 'notre frère,' paradoxically speaks through the categories of racial and national consciousness.[40]

---

[40] Title of Fanon's obituary printed in the FLN organ, El Moudjahid, December 21, 1961 (vol. 88), cover of obituary reproduced in Peter Geismar, Fanon (New York: The Dial Press, 1971), 134–6.

In the Americas, Fanon might be productively compared with José Martí and W.E.B. Du Bois, intellectuals and activists of socialist bent who spoke both nationally, in manifestoes for Cuban independence and African American emancipation, and transnationally, in denunciations of American and global imperialism and in imagined communities such as Martí's 'Nuestra América' and Du Bois's 'darker peoples of the world.' Martí and Du Bois elaborate a foundational notion of a distinctively American, prototypically 'post-colonial' notion of hybridity through the seemingly atavistic expressive mediums of nationhood and the autochthonous, of racial gift and racial striving. Martí's 1891 essay, 'Nuestra América' (Our America) identified two Americas, one to the North, imperialist and capitalist; and one to the South, economically exploited, culturally colonized, and ignorant of its own reality. Martí describes the cultural dependency of 'Nuestra América' through the nineteenth-century iconography of degeneration: 'We were a masquerade in English trousers, Parisian vest, North American jacket, and Spanish hat . . . [w]e were all epaulets and tunics in countries that came into the world with hemp sandals on their feet and headbands for hats.'[41] Against this continental dandy, a harlequin of foreign models, Martí envisions a new revolutionary culture whose watchword will be not imitation but creation, a culture in which the 'natural man' conquers 'the foreign book' (141). In a figure of speech that literalizes the discourse of the hybrid in the projects of Caribbean and Latin American nationalism, Martí proclaims '[l]et the world be grafted [*injértese*] on our republics; but the trunk [*tronco*] must be our own' (143). Against the artifices of clothing and horticulture a continental body emerges that is at once hybrid in form and indigenous in roots. The indigenous here refers to the original Indian inhabitants of the Americas and their descendants, to the African slaves brought to the New World and their descendants, and to *mestizos* and white creoles, all of whose intertwinings make of Martí's America a place where the old notion of biologically differentiated 'races' belongs on the 'library-shelf,' not in the national imaginary (150).[42]

[41] José Martí, 'Our America,' in *The America of José Martí*, trans. Juan de Onís (New York: Noonday Press, 1953), 138–51, 146.

[42] For another statement that pits ideas of race and racial difference against the attainment of continental and specifically national (Cuban) well-being, see Martí's 1893 essay, 'My Race,' also reprinted in *The America of José Martí*, 308–12. José David Saldívar discusses Martí as cultural critic in *The Dialectics of Our America*; also see Sylvia Molloy's useful contextualization of Martí within *fin-de-siècle* Latin American *modernismo*'s fascination with decadence in 'Too

There are powerful resonances between Martí's figuration of specifically Cuban and broadly Latin American independence through the indigenous hybrid and Du Bois's vision of African Americans' emancipatory struggle. Speaking a generation after the end of slavery, in an 1897 address to the newly-formed American Negro Academy entitled 'The Conservation of Races,' Du Bois claimed of African Americans: 'their destiny is not a servile imitation of Anglo-Saxon culture, but a stalwart originality which shall unswervingly follow Negro ideals.'[43] Insisting both that '[w]e are Americans' and that 'we are Negroes, members of a vast historic race,' Du Bois impossibly welds national to racial identity in the midst of an era known for the vast and terrorizing lengths it went to in order to preserve a categorical distance between the two for Black subjects.[44] In an adroit, Douglass-like hollowing out of the very notion of national identity, Du Bois suggests that it is the former slaves who are the most American of citizens; '[w]e are that people whose subtle sense of song has given America its only American music, its only American fairy tales.'

The elaboration of a liberationist agenda couched in the terms of racial character and racial 'gift' is one that recurs throughout Du Bois's work, from The Souls of Black Folk with its catalogue of African American song, story, and toil and its demand, '[a]re not these gifts worth the giving? . . . Would America have been America without her Negro people?' (215), to pan-Africanist histories such as The Negro and its derivative volumes, The Gift of Black Folk: The Negroes in the Making of America (1924) and Black Folk Then and Now (1939). Du Bois's strange 1928 novel Dark Princess presents an exemplary case in which the global proletarian struggle of the 'darker peoples of the world' is visualized through the romantic lens of old-style races. The committee of the 'darker peoples' includes aristocratic, cosmopolitan Chinese, Egyptians, Arabs, Japanese, and Indians, towards whom the Arabs and

Wilde for Comfort: Desire and Ideology in Fin-de-Siècle Spanish America,' Social Text 31/21 (1992), 187–201.

[43] W.E.B. Du Bois, 'The Conservation of Races,' in W.E.B. Du Bois on Sociology and the Black Community, ed. Dan S. Green and Edwin D. Driver (Chicago and London: University of Chicago Press, 1978), 238–49, 243–4. See Appiah's 'Illusions of Race' in In My Father's House, 28–46 for an elegant diagnosis of the paradox whereby Du Bois's address rejects biological concepts of race only to sneak them back in the guise of a culturalist discourse of blood and heritage.

[44] W.E.B. Du Bois, The Souls of Black Folk (New York: Penguin, 1989), 215.

Japanese prove deeply distrustful and duplicitous as they endeavor to break off the interest that the socialist-inclined Indian Princess Kautilya has taken in the plight of the 'Negro race both in Africa and America' generally and in the African American expatriate Mathew Towns specifically, following Mathew's rendition of a slave spiritual before a meeting of the committee.[45] The messianic birth of Mathew and Kautilya's son, a blending of cultures and nations that 'changes the world,' begs inclusion in any study of American figurations of hybrid identity.[46]

Du Bois presents an intriguing case for post-colonial criticism because of the extraordinary breadth of his work, ranging from his dissertation on the suppression of the slave trade and early sociological studies of African Americans designed to counter the myths of scientific racism, to later work for civil rights at home as a founding member of the National Association for the Advanced of Colored People (NAACP) and for the rights of national self-determination abroad as an organizer of the major pan-African Congresses and a supporter of worldwide socialist struggle. Does Du Bois's American provenance unfit him for post-colonial paradigms or does his internationalism purchase him an exceptional entry? What would it mean to locate Du Bois on post-colonial theoretical territory? Such a placing would have to work through the relationship between the institution of slavery, whose historical conditions and social and cultural legacies were so central to the early stages of Du Bois' intellectual project, and the institutions of colonialism and imperialism, whose global sway increasingly occupied him. Such a placing would also have to take into consideration the fact that like Fanon and like Martí, Du Bois was both intellectual and an activist, both a theoretician and a revolutionary. Such an overlapping of identities, in its troubling of powerful dichotomies and in its boundary-crossing creation of new political formations and new politics, may in fact serve contemporary scholars of post-

[45] W.E.B. Du Bois, *Dark Princess* (Jackson, MS: University Press of Mississippi, 1995), 21.

[46] Ibid., 308. See Gilroy's reading of this scene as 'an image of hybridity and intermixture that is especially valuable because it gives no ground to the suggestion that cultural fusion involves betrayal, loss, corruption, or dilution ... This is not the fusion of two purified essences but rather a meeting of two heterogenous multiplicities that in yielding themselves up to each other create something durable and entirely appropriate to troubled anti-colonial times': 'Du Bois, Germany, and the Politics of (Dis)placement,' in *The Black Atlantic*, 111–45, 144–5.

coloniality both as an investigative object and as a model for our own praxis. The question of Du Bois's and (I extrapolate unwisely) American post-coloniality also demands a more complete indexing of historical practices of racialized and ethnicized subordination in the United States, including the enslavement of Africans, the genocide of Native Americans, the dispossession of Mexican Americans, and the exploitation of ethnic European and East Asian immigrants – a list that does not begin to address the complex domestic and transnational patterns of labor and poverty in the contemporary United States.

In contrast to critics such as Omi and Winant, and Mani and Frankenberg, who question the applicability of 'internal colonization' theses and post-colonial paradigms to the United States,[47] Christine MacLeod argues that a shared history of rupture, subordination, and marginalization connects African Americans and post-colonial peoples. She calls on post-colonial theory to allow its internal debates to be 'clarified, interrogated, sharpened, enriched' through an engagement with African American texts. The study of these convergences for MacLeod necessitates, among other things, analysis of the 'intersections' between European Orientalism and 'America's self-fashioning through an Africanist mythology,' and 'the theorizing of hybridity as against the romantic or strategic appeals of "race retrieval" and cultural nationalism.' Du Bois's *The Souls of Black Folk*, Richard Wright's *Native Son*, and Ralph Ellison's *Invisible Man* become for MacLeod paradigmatic instances of a distinctly post-colonial yet characteristically African American discourse of doubleness, splitting, and hybridity.[48] A text like Du Bois's *Souls* is clearly hybrid in its famous figure of 'double consciousness' as well as in the generic 'polyphony' of its form, encompassing sociological statistics and the sorrow songs of slaves, ethnography and autobiography, polemic and elegy, parable and historical analysis.[49]

---

[47] See footnote 14.

[48] Christine MacLeod, 'Black American Literature and the Postcolonial Debate,' *The Yearbook of English Studies* 27 (1997), 51–65, 58.

[49] Writes Du Bois: 'It is a peculiar sensation, this double-consciousness, this sense of always looking at one's self through the eyes of others, of measuring one's soul by the tape of a world that looks on in amused contempt and pity. One ever feels his twoness – an American, a Negro; two souls, two thoughts, two unreconciled strivings; two warring ideals in one dark body, whose dogged strength alone keeps it from being torn asunder. The history of the American Negro is the history of this strife – this longing to attain self-conscious manhood, to merge his double self into a better and truer self. In this merging he wishes neither of the older selves to be lost' (5). On the mixed generic composition of *Souls* see Gilroy's *The Black Atlantic*, 115.

But *Souls'* hybridity, like that of *Dark Princess*, is also deeply imbricated with, rather than easily situated 'against,' the conceptual categories of race, culture, and nation. All of these must be read doubly, both with recognition of the nineteenth-century narratives of slavery, colonialism, racism, and empire in which these categories are embedded, and with an ear for the ways in which Du Bois's use of these categories resonates with twentieth-century struggles against racial injustice and global imperialism. Both *Souls'* concluding image of African Americans as a community who 'have woven ourselves with the very warp and woof of this nation' (215) and the golden son of Mathew and Kautilya, baptized by a black preacher reading from Revelation and blessed by Hindu, Buddhist, and Muslim holy men, suggest intermixture, but in somewhat different registers. Whereas *Souls* expresses the pathos of unrecognized kinship and unlawfully withheld equality, *Dark Princess* celebrates the romantic promise of a changed world in which particular identities (race, nation, culture, religion) have not been transcended or transmuted so much as brought together.

Constraints of time and space have made my reading of a possible genealogy of the hybrid in the Americas unfortunately telegraphic, singling out figures and concepts in Equiano and Douglass, Du Bois and Martí that demand closer reading, clearer situation within their respective national and transnational contexts, and more elaborate contextualization within the New World discourse on slavery, the Latin American discourse of *mestizaje*, the Caribbean discourse of *metissage*, and the African American discourses of cultural assimilation, biological mixing, and racial passing. With regard to race and nation, the work must be delicate, both historicizing these categories within the nineteenth century's bio-genetic discourse of blood and soil and its progressivist plots of savagery and civilization, and locating the moments where they appear to break, if only partially, out of that set of contexts and into others. In invoking Equiano and Douglass, Du Bois and Martí, I do not mean to unmoor them from their respective disciplinary homes within the study of slavery, African American studies, Latin American studies and an increasingly hemispherically mapped, transnationally concerned American studies, so that I may tow them into provenance of 'the post-colonial.' To suggest that each of these texts is primarily or paradigmatically 'post-colonial' would be to parody the very englobing discourse that post-colonial studies is presumably in the business of unpacking. Without then claiming these texts *for* 'the post-colonial' I would nonetheless like to suggest that they speak in timely and important ways *to* 'the post-colonial' and its academic partisans. To the extent that these four local histories of the hybrid find expression in the modalities of race and nation, they remind us that to imagine, as contemporary post-colonial studies sometimes seems to do, that we can simply choose one (hybrid) model of identity over another (particularist) one, or posit strict chronological passages from the latter to the former, is to forget precisely the ways in which these conceptual categories are collectively bound to one another and frequently serve to narrate one another.

IV

On the terrain of contemporary post-colonial studies, South Africa beckons critics particularly insistently to reject dichotomized methodologies and to try to account for the lived intersections of different paradigms of identity, both the classificatory minutiae of apartheid's racialism and the hybridizing project of the new 'Rainbow Nation.' Currently, South Africa finds itself in the difficult position of at once revisiting, undoing, and reinventing its national identity. This is evident, for example, in the gradual efforts of government ministries to reverse the inequitable distribution of land, resources, housing, education, and social services that made, in a famous phrase of the South African Communist Party, 'Non-White South Africa . . . the colony of White South Africa itself,' and in the Truth and Reconciliation Commission's provision of a forum for national confession and national testimony regarding the crimes of the past. Nicholas Visser has suggested that the internal colony thesis, or 'colonialism-of-a-special-type' (CST) as it came to be called in South African political analysis of the 1960s, 70s, and 80s, finds an 'interesting reprise' in the more recent (mis)appropriation by South African academics of post-colonial theory. Like CST, Visser argues, post-colonial theory posits a monolithic colonialism at work in apartheid, and like CST post-colonial theory essentializes 'race' as the *sine qua non* of South African identity and subjectivity, thereby imputing to South Africa's non-white population a uniformity of oppression that has fundamentally evaded the question of class or, in the case of CST, deferred it to a (now bypassed) 'second stage' of socialism following national and racial liberation.[50] In a similar vein, Kelwyn Sole criticizes South African post-colonialists for a liberal

[50] Visser, 'Postcoloniality of a Special Type,' 80–1, 86, 92–3.

humanist focus on highly essentialized categories of race, ethnicity, and culture which effectively downplays and displaces class.[51] Both Visser and Sole suggest that hegemonic post-colonial studies in its South African variety does not ignore race so much as obsessively fixate on it as a guarantor that 'difference' is being addressed and that the distinctiveness of formerly marginalized communities is being registered in some multiculturalist version of academic discourse.[52] For many South African intellectuals and activists schooled in the ANC's non-racialist tradition, to speak of race now is tantamount to the retention and promulgation of old apartheid classificatory categories.[53] Not to speak of race and ethnicity, however, is to risk elision of apartheid's legacies; it is to commit that very error of which 'the post-colonial' is so frequently found guilty, namely the premature announcement of the end of a system of domination and the erasure of its contemporary traces. The strange place of the idea of race in an emergent non-racial state, where it is at once deeply and structurally embedded and for some citizens politically and ideologically unthinkable, captures some of what is unique or 'special' about South Africa's present state and the questions it poses to metropolitan-based post-colonial and cultural studies.[54]

South Africa by some accounts has become post-colonial several

---

[51] Sole, 'South Africa Passes the Posts,' especially 127–32, 147.

[52] Visser's and Sole's arguments, while they might seem baldly to contradict my own suggestion that dominant post-colonial studies elides questions of race, in fact serve to further clarify the nature of that elision. I have called here not so much for post-colonial studies to 'see' race (which Visser and Sole claim it already does) as for a fundamental change in *how* it sees race, as a category not in itself but in mobile relation with other categories of identity and structures of social relations, produced by distinct historical institutions and political formations, subject to a range of ideological deployments and transformations.

[53] For background see Julie Frederikse, *The Unbreakable Thread: Non-Racialism in South Africa* (Johannesburg: Ravan Press, 1990), as well as Gail M. Gerhart's *Black Power in South Africa: The Evolution of an Ideology* (Berkeley: University of California Press, 1979).

[54] For work that engages these questions see Ran Greenstein, 'Racial Formation: Towards a Comparative Study of Collective Identities in South Africa and the United States,' *Social Dynamics* 19.2 (1993), 1–29; Laura Chrisman, 'Appropriate Appropriations? Developing Cultural Studies in South Africa,' in *Transgressing Boundaries: New Directions in the Study of Culture in Africa*, ed. Brenda Cooper and Andrew Steyn (Cape Town and Columbus: University of Cape Town Press and Ohio University Press, 1996), 184–95. For perspectives on the place of post-colonial theory in South Africa, see essays in *Current Writing* 5:2 (1994), and David Johnson, 'Importing Metropolitan Post-Colonials,' *Current Writing* 6:1 (1994), 73–85.

times already, each time for a distinctly different population, with the creation of Union in 1910, with the victory of the Afrikaner-based National Party and the birth of the apartheid state in 1948, with the declaration of Republic rather than Commonwealth status in 1960, and of course most famously with the 1994 transition. South Africa thus questions the prevailing narrative of post-coloniality that posits a single break into that state of being, while it also questions models of the post-colonial as a diasporic formation in which culture and cultural subjects (too frequently, cosmopolitan intellectual cultural subjects) travel, hybridize, and transform. In the South African case, this contestatory process was and is framed within the space of the national, not outside it. The legacies of the population movements engendered by Dutch slavery in the seventeenth and eighteenth centuries, British colonial expansion and indentured servitude in the nineteenth century, and Afrikaner racial capitalism and coerced migrant labor in the twentieth century have combined to create a present-day nation containing a heterogenous population with both distinct and common claims to justice. At the present time, the South African state finds itself trying to foster the creation of genuinely national culture, into which the particular cultural, linguistic, and ethnic identities of various groups will not be subsumed, but over which they will equally not, any one of them, dominate. Even as the 'new South Africa' reconstitutes a nation in which official discourse on 'culture' strains to do the work of differentiation and unification ('one nation, many cultures' reads a popular ANC slogan), another narrative plays out on the nation's borders where the many migrants and refugees find little chance of inclusion and are subject to serious human rights abuses.[55] Many but not all of these refugees come from frontline states such as Mozambique and Angola, in whose civil wars the former South African regime played a central part.

   I hope that these local sitings (they are too cursory to merit the term specifications) of the workings of colonial capitalist rule, post-colonial state politics, and neo-colonial capitalism in South Africa suggest some of the conceptual malleability as well as the resurgent fixity of such constructs as race and nation. Without an extended discussion of the various ways in which these phenomena are being discussed in South

---

[55] See the account of the recent Human Rights Watch Report on human rights abuses committed by the South African government against undocumented immigrants in 'US Human Rights Report Guns for SA Government,' *Weekly Mail and Guardian* (March 24, 1998).

Africa now, and of the effects that discussion is having on the formation of post-colonial studies in South Africa, any claim to find in these observations the occasion of comparative post-colonial studies must ring false. Apartheid, like colonialism and slavery, marks the limits of a constitutively western discourse of humanism, modernity, and progress. To place these systems of racialized domination in some kind of concert with one another is not to claim them for post-colonial scholarship but rather to place that scholarship in a position to rethink itself, to reconnect perhaps with the critical analysis of the changing constructs of race and nation as they delineate both the workings of subordinating systems and the oppositional struggles against them.

V

The academic dissemination of an oppositional viewpoint variously called post-colonial, post-independence, Third Worldist, materialist, anti-colonialist and anti-imperialist, anti-neo-colonialist and anti-neo-imperialist, or non-metropolitan, while it by no means holds a conceptual monopoly on the issues it anatomizes, has nonetheless reshaped the way in which we think about such potent categories as power, resistance, culture, and identity. Over the past several years, there has been significant debate over the extent to which the specifically 'post-colonial' variant of this viewpoint effectively displaces the other, more historically situated terms. In addition, attention has been devoted to examining the premises of post-colonial theory and its political consequences,[56] among which we must now count the increasingly legitimized institutional presence of post-colonial studies. The latter problem is one whose ironies would not have been lost on Marx (Groucho not Karl): if they want us in the academic club, perhaps we don't want to be members. Put more seriously, as post-colonial studies has become academic fashion and therefore academic necessity, reflected in the rapidly growing advertisements for specialists in post-colonial or 'world' literatures, we would do well to question the ways in which academic institutions interpellate and situate our work and ourselves. If, as Arif Dirlik claims, the set of critical themes that post-colonial criticism claims as

---

[56] Shohat, 'Notes on the Post-Colonial'; Brennan, *Cosmopolitanism Now*; Parry, 'Problems' and 'The Postcolonial: Conceptual Category or Chimera'; Ahmad, *In Theory* and 'The Politics of Literary Post-coloniality.'

its own in fact predate the contemporary currency of that term, that is to say if post-colonialism shares its concerns with other historical eras, political moments, geographical locales, and disciplinary discourses, then we cannot afford to write our disciplinary history (and future) simply in the terms of self-reflection.[57]

We should be constructing a field of inquiry that takes seriously the work of transnational comparison and of historicization, a field that mediates methodologically between global and local visions. The analysis of contemporary and historical post-colonial formations within the United States and, more broadly, the Americas, and of the degree to which they can and cannot be understood through colonial and imperial paradigms should become a more common part of post-colonial studies in the American academy. Such grounding in one's own political contexts, which we have come to expect of and even to criticize in those rather monolithic figures known as 'post-colonial intellectuals,' beckons closer to home. These locations and the disciplinary alliances they might entail, for example with ethnic studies departments where 'internal colonization' theses have long been debated, could help to create a post-colonial studies more aware of its own history and more cognizant of its institutional functions, complicities, and responsibilities. We should be learning from our colleagues; diversifying our sense of who fits within the category of a post-colonial hire, perhaps sharing appointments and certainly exchanging lectures and courses with departments of ethnic studies, history, anthropology, sociology, economics, political science, geography. At the same time, we should also be wary of englobing tendencies.

Stuart Hall, speaking several years ago in Illinois at a major cultural studies conference, registered his somewhat uneasy admiration of the institutional resources that many US universities have thrown behind this 'new' field and warned his audience that despite its growing popularity, 'cultural studies isn't every damn thing.'[58] I find myself worrying that post-colonial studies is on the verge of becoming every damn thing, serving as the sign for oppositional criticism in all modes and rendering colonial and imperial analogies, as well as invocations of hybridity, intermixture, and transculturation, practically obligatory

---

[57] Dirlik, 'The Postcolonial Aura,' 329.
[58] Stuart Hall, 'Cultural Studies and its Theoretical Legacies,' in *Cultural Studies*, ed. Lawrence Grossberg, Cary Nelson, Paula A. Treichler (New York and London: Routledge, 1992), 277–94, 292.

in contemporary criticism. But if the institutional apotheosis of post-colonial studies has its dangers, it also has its possibilities. We need to maintain the academic space and transformative potential to which this field has gained access in the forms of courses, programs of study, job hires, and publishing trends. At the same time we should challenge and resist the tendency such space has to implode into a constricted canon of representative texts, or to explode into a globe-spanning array of literary and cultural production that threatens to make dilettantes of us all. At once too vast and too confined, post-colonial studies' problem seems one of erratic scale as much as of misguided temporality. The very range and diversity of post-colonial curricula, often bemoaned by practitioners and critics alike, may be a strength as Gayatri Spivak suggests in calling for the removal of the 'single author course from the English major curriculum' and the subsequent creation of an academic space in which 'undergraduates will have their lives changed perhaps by a sense of the diversity of the new canon and the unacknowledged power play involved in securing the old.'[59]

Through a remapped history of post-colonial studies of the sort I have here attempted we might begin to situate such governing terms as difference, hybridity, heterogeneity, local particularism, and global cosmopolitanism in a historical, geo-political, socio-cultural, and intellectual context rather longer than that of the past two decades of critical theory. A reconsideration of the function of the categories of race and nation within post-colonial studies entails neither the reasserted critical hegemony of two isolated terms nor the unproblematized 'return' to some originary reservoir of identitarian politics. Rather, such a project attempts to carve out an arena of inquiry through which we may better understand the ideological complexity and historical malleability of race and nation themselves. We may also come to understand the processes of negotiation, articulation, and rupture that define the many contemporary social movements and literary/cultural expressions that speak sometimes in the voice of race and nation, often against it or 'after' it, but always somehow in its shadow. In that shadow may lie some light, for in trying to decipher the murky processes of affiliation and contestatory politics that are at once old and new, post-colonial criticism may also come to reconsider its imperative to divide between what is past and what

---

[59] Gayatri Chakravorty Spivak, 'The Making of Americans, The Teaching of English, and the Future of Culture Studies,' New Literary History 24 (1990), 781–98, 783.

is present, what belongs to it and what can be banished. All of this by way of saying that disciplinary histories never begin quite where you think they do, and what you leave out of them has a way of returning.

Listening to the Subaltern: Postcolonial Studies and the Neocolonial Poetics of Subaltern States

FERNANDO CORONIL

Postcolonial Studies and Latin America

THE GROWING FIELD of postcolonial studies has been developed in the metropolitan centers by scholars working on northern European colonialism in Asia and Africa. Latin America and the Caribbean, characterized by a much longer entanglement with colonialism and its aftermath, figures only tangentially in this field.[1] This exclusion has meant a neglect of neocolonialism, imperialism and internal colonialism, central concerns in the Americas since the first quarter of the nineteenth century, when Haiti became the first independent state produced by a slave revolution, and most of Latin America achieved political independence from Spain through wars of independence which were in some respects also social wars. These concerns with new forms of postcolonial subjection were intensified by interrelated events: Cuba's truncated independence in 1898 after a devastating thirty-year struggle that entailed a confrontation at once with declining Spanish colonialism, emerging US imperialism, and persisting domestic racial and class privilege; the 1898 annexation of Puerto Rico by the United States, establishing a country which has an ambiguous and contradictory status as a 'free' and 'associated' state ('el estado libre asociado'); and the US-backed separation of Panama from Colombia in 1903, which created a nation designed to be the location of a US-controlled canal. In each country of the region post-independence projects to achieve 'modern nationhood' have made evident their limits in the context of shifting postcolonial power relations.

This 'failure of the nation to come into its own,' to borrow Ranajit Guha's evocative phrase to address the limits of nationhood in postcolonial India, has led in Latin America and the Caribbean to an extraordinary tradition of thought, embodied in academic scholarship

[1] For an insightful discussion of this neglect in the current literature, see Hulme (1996)

37

as well as the arts (popular and elite), that constitutes a monumental collective reflection on this failure. Drawing on this tradition – particularly its reflections on the relationship between shifting modalities of postcolonial imperial hegemony and state transformations – I seek in this essay to explore forms of subjection associated with neoliberal globalization and modes of analysis that could oppose them. In so doing, I also hope to contribute to the field of postcolonial studies from a Latin American perspective.

Rethinking the Subaltern

On February 27, 1989, large numbers of people took to the streets in Venezuela's major cities in protest against worsening economic conditions. By the end of the day, several hundred thousand people in Caracas and many thousands in other major cities had participated in protests which included rioting and looting. Popular anger was triggered by a 100 percent price increase in state-owned gasoline, which had led to the doubling of fares for public transportation. This step, taken to bring the price of domestic gasoline in line with world-market gasoline prices, was one of the initial measures implemented by the three-week-old government of President Carlos Andrés Pérez as part of a state policy shift from protectionism – a deeply entrenched distributionist system fueled by abundant petro-dollars – toward a free-market economic model designed in accordance with International Monetary Fund requirements for debtor nations. After thirty years of oil-supported democratic stability and party control over popular mobilization, the populace was believed to be incapable of such an independent expression of will. Having erroneously assumed the passivity of the popular sectors, the startled government reacted to their activism with unprecedented repression. Several thousand soldiers were airlifted to Caracas from the interior. The armed forces of the state opened fire on people in the barrios and on the streets, killing several hundred.[2] Lasting five days, this episode was the largest and most severely repressed protest against austerity measures not only in Venezuelan history, but in contemporary Latin America.

[2] The official figure is 276. Definitive figures are difficult to establish: unofficial estimates of the death toll made by journalists and human rights organizations have been reduced from around 1,000 (at the time of the riots) to 400.

On March 1, during the third day of rioting, the public waited anxiously for the government to make a long-delayed televised announcement to the nation. Minister of the Interior Alejandro Izaguirre, a seasoned politician who had frequently served as the acting head of state, appeared before the cameras. Much to the public's shock, he muttered, 'I can't, I can't,' and stopped speaking. Radio and television stations immediately interrupted the broadcast without explanation. One of the networks aired Disney cartoons for the remaining time that had been reserved by the government. The state, ordinarily the central source of authoritative public speech, suddenly appeared speechless.

This incident reveals in a flash that state speech – not only its form or content, but its very condition of possibility – cannot be taken for granted. More fundamentally, this moment of state speechlessness makes dramatically visible the problematic nature of what typically appears as its obverse – subaltern political speech – and raises questions about subalternity in general: its different modalities of agency, its various modes of expression, and the possibility of representing them.

I want to explore these broad questions by focusing on some specific instances of state action and discourse in Venezuela during a turning point in the current period of neoliberal globalization. I do so not in order to shift the usual focus of subaltern studies from social actors that are at the bottom of social hierarchies towards ones that occupy higher positions, but to offer a relational conception of subalternity that expands the range of its subjects and focuses on their constitution in shifting relations of subjection. In her influential article 'Can the Subaltern Speak?' Gayatri Spivak (1988a) problematizes the production and retrieval of subaltern speech (in this case, as discussed below, the words and actions of Bhuvaneswari Badhuri, a young Indian woman) in light of its dependence on dominant discursive fields, which constitute subaltern subjects, define their modalities of expression, and structure the positions from which they speak and are heard.

Here I want to address the problem Spivak has so provocatively and productively raised in order to advance a different approach to subalternity. Spivak's aim is, in her words, 'to learn to speak to (rather than listen to or speak for) the historically muted subject of the non-elite' (Ibid.: 271). While I appreciate her insights into the politics of representation and her reticence to speak for subjected others, I seek to explore modes of listening to subaltern subjects and of interpreting what I hear. If any epistemological position entails a politics, my aim in this discussion is to learn to speak to the subject of subalternity in ways that may contribute to overcoming the conditions that make subalternity possible. By treating subalternity as a hetero-geneous social field encompassing multiple social subjects, and by regarding their relations of difference and identity as the condition for a shared politics, I wish to examine modes of conceptualizing and representing the subaltern that counter rather than confirm the silencing effect of domination.

Spivak, by means of an extended discussion of sati (or suttee) – the practice of self-immolation by Indian widows on their husbands' pyres – presents as emblematic of the subaltern the case of a political activist who sought to communicate her personal predicament through her suicide, but whose communication was foiled by the codes of patriarchy and colonialism in which her actions were inevitably inscribed. Spivak depicts her situation in the following terms:

> A young woman of sixteen or seventeen, Bhuvaneswari Bhaduri, hanged herself in her father's modest apartment in North Calcutta in 1926. The suicide was a puzzle since, as Bhuvaneswari was menstruating at the time, it was clearly not a case of illicit pregnancy. Nearly a decade later, it was discovered that she was a member of one of the many groups involved in the armed struggle for Indian independence. She had finally been entrusted with a political assassination. Unable to confront the task and yet aware of the practical need for trust, she killed herself . . . Bhuvaneswari had known that her death would be diagnosed as the outcome of illegitimate passion. She had therefore waited for the onset of menstruation. While waiting, Bhuvaneswari, the brahmacarini who was no doubt looking forward to a good wifehood, perhaps rewrote the social text of sati-suicide in an interventionist way. (Ibid.: 307)

Despite Bhaduri's precautions, her death is remembered by her relatives (her nieces) as 'a case of illicit love,' and the meaning of her act thus seems to have been lost to history, although it is not clear, given the nature of the evidence provided, whether Spivak was uniquely able to retrieve it (Ibid.: 308). Since Bhaduri's actions are not only inscribed but read in terms of the dominant codes of British imperialism and Indian patriarchy, Spivak concludes, provocatively, that 'the subaltern cannot speak' (Ibid.).

Her conclusion is preceded by a critique of Foucault and Deleuze, through which she discusses the dangers of reinscribing imperial assumptions in colonial studies, and of Antonio Gramsci's and Ranajit

Guha's treatments of subalternity, in which her main focus is Guha's analysis of the social structure of postcolonial societies by means of a 'dynamic stratification grid':

Elite: { 1. Dominant foreign groups.
          2. Dominant indigenous groups on the all-India level.
       3. Dominant indigenous groups at the regional and local levels.
       4. The terms 'people' and 'subaltern classes' have been used as synonymous throughout this note. The social groups and elements included in this category represent *the demographic difference between the total Indian population and all those whom we have described as the 'ehte.'*

(Ibid.: 284 [Guha's emphases])

Guha's grid is built upon the assumption that subalternity resides in 'the people,' taken as an undifferentiated subject. In terms of this grid, the intermediate groups between the elite and the people, the 'dominant indigenous groups at the regional and local levels' (number 3), are particularly problematic because they can be either dominant or dominated, depending on situational considerations. As Guha says, 'The same class or element which was dominant in one area . . . could be among the dominated in another. This could and did create many ambiguities and contradictions in attitudes and alliances, especially among the lowest strata of the rural gentry, impoverished landlords, rich peasants and upper-middle-class peasants all of whom belonged, *ideallly speaking*, to the category of people or subaltern classes' (Ibid. [Guha's emphases]). Given this conceptualization of the intermediate groups within the project of studying the subaltern, Spivak notes that for Guha the 'task of research' is 'to investigate, identify, and measure the *specific* nature and degree of the *deviation* of [the] elements [constituting item 3] from the ideal and situate it historically' (Ibid.: 285 [Guha's emphases]).

Noting the essentialist and taxonomic character of this program, Spivak emphasizes the fact that 'the object of the group's investigation, in this case not even of the people as such but of the floating buffer zone of the regional elite-subaltern, is a *deviation* from an *ideal* – the people or subaltern – which is itself defined as a difference from the elite' (Ibid. [Spivak's emphases]). After making these observations, Spivak leaves the problematic 'buffer zone group' behind and moves on to problematize the research of item 4: 'the people,' or 'subaltern classes,' the *ideal* itself.

In her provocative but complicated discussion of the subaltern as female, she seems to be arguing that the subaltern's voice/consciousness cannot be retrieved, and that analysis should indicate this impossibility by charting the positions from which the subaltern speaks, but 'cannot be heard or read' (Ibid.: 308). As one of Spivak's interpreters has argued:

> Rather than speak for a lost consciousness that cannot be recovered, a paternalistic activity at best, the critic can point to the place of woman's disappearance as an *aporia*, a blind-spot where understanding and knowledge is blocked. Complicating the assumption that the gendered subaltern is a homogeneous entity whose voice can be simply retrieved, Spivak demonstrates the paradoxical contradictions of the discourses which produce such *aporia* in the place of subject-positions, showing that the *sati* herself is at best presented with the non-choice of the robber's 'your money or your life!' 'Voice' is of little use in this situation. (Young 1990: 64)

Spivak's assertion that the subaltern cannot speak has been pervasively read as 'an expression of terminal epistemological and political pessimism' (Lowe, Rosenthal, and Silliman 1990: 83). Yet in a subsequent interview, saying that she had been misunderstood, Spivak claimed that her purpose had been to counter the impulse to solve the problem of political subjectivity by romanticizing the subaltern. Instead of treating the subaltern as an unproblematic unified subject, she would apply to the subaltern 'all the complications of "subject production" which are applied to us' (Spivak 1990: 90). While this seems eminently reasonable – except that she presupposes and reproduces a questionable polarity between 'we' (dominant) and 'they' (subaltern) – her next proposal is disconcerting, for Spivak suggests using the term 'subaltern for everything that is different from organized resistance', justifying this usage by building on Guha's introduction to the first volume of Ranajit Guha's *Subaltern Studies* where

> he is making an analysis of how a colonial society is structured, and what space can be spoken of as the subaltern space. There is a space in post-imperial arenas which is displaced from empire – nation exchange. Where one sees the 'emancipated bourgeoisie,' 'organized labor,' 'organized left movements,' 'urban radicalism,' the disenfranchised 'women's arena' (these words are all used in quotes), all of this is constituted within that empire-nation exchange, reversing it in many different kinds of ways. But in post-imperialist societies

there is a vast arena which is not necessarily accessible to that kind of exchange. It is that space that one calls subaltern. The romantic notion that the subaltern as subaltern can speak is totally undermined by the fact that the real effort is to pull them into national agency with the sanctions that are already there. (Ibid.: 90–1)

It seems to me that with this move Spivak has in effect homogenized and pushed the subaltern out of the realm of political exchange, beyond 'national agency.' The ambiguities and contradictions in the notion of the subaltern, which were sharply visible in Guha's intermediate category (the 'dominant indigenous groups at the regional and local levels'), seems to be resolved here by the subaltern's relegation to the margins and transformation into an outsider, an Other.

Thus, building on Foucault's approval of nominalism in *The History of Sexuality*, Spivak says, 'To that extent, the subaltern is the name of the place which is so displaced from what made me and the organized resister, that to have it speak is like Godot arriving on a bus. We want it to disappear as a name so that we can all speak' (Ibid.: 91). If I read her correctly, I take her to mean that the subaltern is mute by definition; subalternity cannot include such active agents as the 'organized resister' or 'me' (since, like Spivak, I can 'speak' literally and metaphorically). Yet if one views subalternity as a heterogenous social field populated by subaltern subjects differently subjected to interrelated power hierarchies, making the subaltern 'disappear as a name' entails the endless process of creating a democratic society – a society without dominance and subalternity, a process that presupposes the recognition of the subaltern as an agent of historical transformation not just despite, but because of, its subalternity at this time. Yet, with this topographic conception, Spivak seems to reconstitute the subaltern not only as a unified subject which cannot speak, but as a mute object – positioned outside agency.

Spivak conceptualizes the subaltern differently in commenting on her own position during her evaluation of the historiographic work of the Subaltern Studies group in India. She says that she is 'progressively inclined . . . to read the retrieval of subaltern consciousness as the charting of what in post-structuralist language [would] be called the subaltern subject-effect.' From this perspective, the subject is metaleptic – an effect substituted for a cause. Her invocation of the strategic use of positivist essentialism appears to be a necessary but theoretically unsatisfactory response to the poststructuralist dissolution of the subject (Spivak 1988b: 12–15). In my view, the problems associated with humanist or structuralist conceptions of sovereign, unified subjects who operate as autonomous causes of historical effects are only mirrored by the poststructuralist conception of fragmented subjects who are or operate as mere effects; a more fruitful conceptualization would be one that overcame the polarization of terms in which this debate is being cast.[3]

As a step in this direction, I propose that we view the subaltern neither as a sovereign-subject that actively occupies a bounded place nor as a vassal-subject that results from the dispersed effects of multiple external determinations, but as an agent of identity construction that participates, under determinate conditions within a field of power relations, in the organization of its multiple positionality and subjectivity. In my view, subalternity is a relational and a relative concept; there are times and places where subjects appear on the social stage as subaltern actors, just as there are times or places in which they play dominant roles. Moreover, at any given time or place, an actor may be subaltern in relation to another, yet dominant in relation to a third. And, of course, there are contexts in which these categories may simply not be relevant. Dominance and subalternity are not inherent, but relational characterizations. Subalternity defines not the being of a subject, but a subjected state of being. Yet because enduring subjection has the effect of fixing subjects into limiting positions, a relational conception of the subaltern requires a double vision that recognizes at one level a common ground among diverse forms of subjection and, at another, the intractable identity of subjects formed within uniquely constraining social worlds. While the first optic opens up a space for establishing links among subordinated subjects (including the analyst who takes a subaltern perspective), the second acknowledges the differentiating and ultimately unshareable effects of specific modalities of subjection.[4] This

[3] Spivak's discussion of the 'subaltern' is developed in yet other directions (which I cannot discuss here) in her response (Spivak 1989) to Benita Parry's (1987) helpful critique of her work. This exchange suggests that a critical awareness of the complicity between imperialism and anthropology should lead not to a rejection of the representation of 'native' voices, but to a critical transformation of anthropology's modes of representing (and of conceptualizing) itself and its objects of study.

[4] This elaboration of my previous understanding of subalternity (1994) owes much to discussions with members of the Grupo de la Playa of the Latin American Subaltern Studies Group in Puerto Rico (March 1996), and especially to Josefina Saldaña's insistence on the radical alterity of subaltern subjects and Alberto Moreiras's suggestion that we use a 'double register' in our approach to the subaltern.

relational and situational view of the subaltern may help anticolonial intellectuals avoid the we/they polarity underlying Spivak's analysis and listen to subaltern voices that speak from variously subordinated positions.

A similar argument concerning the relational character of subalternity which underlines its significance for the study of gender, has been developed by Gail Hershatter who asks: 'What happens if we allow generously for a relational component of subaltern status, so that we can highlight the extent to which people were constituted as subalterns only in relations to others (sometimes several sets of others)?' While in her answer to this question she argues that from this perspective 'the workings of gender become easier to figure all across the class spectrum,' one could generalize her observation and propose that it also makes more visible the workings of other markers of identity, such as race, ethnicity, religion, or nationality, and not just 'across the class spectrum,' but in their mutual interactions, illuminating, in turn, the process of class formation itself. And while this inclusivity risks homogenizing or diluting subalternity, I would endorse as well her observation that 'this inclusive definition of subaltern is emphatically not meant to suggest that all oppressions (or resistances) are equal, that everyone is a subaltern in the same way.' Her hope, which I share, 'is not to render oppression uniform and thus somehow less onerous, but rather to trace the ways that oppressions can be stacked, doubled, intertwined' (1993: 112).[5]

From this perspective, I want to discuss next subaltern speech as it is articulated at the very center of 'peripheral' nations. Drawing my examples from a larger investigation in which I have sought to listen to dominant as well as subaltern discourses by contextualizing them within a historical and cultural field marked by neocolonial relations (Coronil and Skurski 1991), I will focus here exclusively on speech articulated by representatives of the state, who are generally seen as 'dominant' actors. In what form, if any, is subalternity expressed in the speech of the state in subaltern nations, the institution that must constitute and represent itself as the locus of sovereignty and autonomy?

---

[5] I find it interesting that we developed similar arguments independently of each other as we sought to apply the insights of Subaltern Studies to 'a less colonial situation' (Hershatter 1993: 104): 'semi-colonial' China, in her case; 'neocolonial' Venezuela, in mine.

State Speech

Like metropolitan states, subaltern states 'speak' – literally and metaphorically – through the languages that constitute them as central sites
of authority, and their multiple forms of speech impact on the daily
lives of people within their societies. As states, they must continually
authorize themselves by producing binding state-ments (regulations,
laws, policies, etc.) whose authority over citizens within a bounded
geographical and political territory rests on a combination of consent
and coercion. Underlying Weber's understanding of the state as the
institution that holds a monopoly on legitimate violence, is the fact
that the state can not only back up its statements with force, but can
deploy violence as its legitimate statement.

Indeed, on March 1, 1989, the Venezuelan state's speechlessness was
only partial. Minister Izaguirre's collapse before the cameras was a
response to the state's 'speech' in the streets: he fainted when he heard
a burst of gunfire outside and realized that the armed forces were
shooting at people – the *pueblo* – the foundation of Venezuelan populist
nationalism. The minister had spent long, sleepless hours analyzing the
situation with other leaders and coming to terms with the decision he
had been about to announce: the state had brought in the army to
restore public order.

The following day, at a different centre of power, another state
representative was quite able to speak of the need to use violence to
ensure order and progress. Gonzalo Barrios, eighty-eight years old, a
founding figure of Venezuelan democracy, leader of the ruling party,
Accion Democractica, and President of the National Congress, made
an important speech to the congress. The day before, Christian
Democrat Rafael Caldera, former President of Venezuela, had delivered
an impassioned address to this same body, urging the nation's leadership to recognize the existence of serious problems and to restore
national unity. Barrios's speech was both a response to this call and a
justification of the measures the government had resolved to take to
enforce public order.

The contrast between Minister Izaguirre's and Senator Barrios's
responses to the crisis highlights not only the opposition between
speech and speechlessness, but also their location on a shared discursive terrain. It is within the context of Izaguirre's silence that I wish
to examine Barrios's speech, so as to illuminate the dynamic relationship between speech and its 'locus of enunciation' (Mignolo 1989)

during changing historical conditions. At this critical juncture in Venezuelan history, the outlines of a reconfigured relationship between state and nation, government and citizenry, became visible. The different responses by these officials to the crisis represent two distinct interventions in this redrawing of Venezuela's identity.

Representing the State

At first glance, Barrios's speech seems like just one more instance of the usual intra-elite dispute over everyday politics. It is difficult to discern from its tone or content, that a crisis is underway, that several hundred people have already been killed, or that the army is at that very moment shooting people in the streets. As Barrios's discourse unfolds, what seems to matter is preventing Caldera from using the crisis to elevate himself and to be recognized as the authoritative interpreter of these events.

Senator Barrios starts by noting that he was glad to have had the opportunity to read Caldera's speech instead of responding to it as he heard it the previous day, for 'it is not the same thing to listen to a speech and to experience the collective emotion that it unleashes as it is to be able to judge it quietly in one's study, reading and rereading some concepts in order to see their hidden intent' (Barrios 1989: 143). Speaking as the tempered voice of reason, Barrios then proceeds to set the record straight by presenting his own interpretation of events. Thus, in the midst of a crisis characterized by the massive, independent intervention of popular sectors in national politics, what this exchange foregrounds is an intra-elite difference of opinion. In its failure to focus either on the actions and voices in the street or even on their armed repression, Barrios's speech embodies the silencing and denial of popular claims on the nation.

This exclusion of the popular sectors is reproduced throughout the speech. In the face of an independent mass action, former President Caldera emphasizes the need for 'leaders to reach out to the *pueblo* in order to channel their feelings toward civic attitudes, toward orderly protest, toward [making] their presence [felt] within the framework of the Constitution and the laws' (Caldera 1989: 136). In his response, Barrios minimizes the importance of popular mobilization by attributing it to the influence of political agitators. Distancing himself from Caldera, he condemns interpretations that explain the recourse to violent action by appeal to the growing frustrations of people faced with worsening living conditions. Just as the command 'thou shall not kill' allows no exceptions, Barrios argues, people should not be permitted to engage in violent actions. Revealingly, Barrios appears not to notice the irony in this case, namely that the commandment is being violated in the streets and barrios by the government, as the army escalates its attack and the death toll reaches several hundred (fewer than ten casualties among government forces resulted from the week of conflict). For Barrios, the popular sectors remain fundamentally faceless.

At this moment of crisis, the public that concerns Barrios is to be found outside Venezuela, in the United States and Europe. He observes that 'it is very rare for the television of these countries to take note of our countries,' particularly if it is a question of reporting happy incidents or facts that elevate us, but it would seem that they rejoice in presenting 'any event, any manifestation, that tends to show us as depressed countries, as primitive cultures' (Barrios 1989: 144). He expresses his regret that these events have shown 'the horror, the primitive, the uncontrollable, from a civilized point of view, of the looting that took place in Caracas' (Ibid.). According to Barrios, this has happened at a time when Venezuela has been demanding more attention from these nations and has managed to overcome 'the prejudices that exist in the developed nations with respect to ourselves' (Ibid.). The day before, Caldera had expressed a similar concern over Venezuela's shattered image in a much-quoted passage of his speech: 'Venezuela has been a kind of pilot country. At this moment it is what North Americans call a "showcase," the display case of Latin American democracy . . . This display case was destroyed by the blows and rocks of the starving people from the Caracas barrios who are being subjected to the iron chains imposed, directly or indirectly, by the IMF' (Caldera 1989: 137). Building on a distinction between 'developed nations' and 'our countries,' both Caldera and Barrios express regret at the negative image of Venezuela now being projected to the developed world.

Caldera's metaphor of Venezuela as a showcase, with its Madison Avenue overtones, had wide appeal partly because it conjured up the familiar image of a gap between the facade of national progress and the lived reality of chronic problems. His speech observed the typical conventions of nationalist rhetoric, including a grandiloquent call to repair the tarnished image of Venezuela as a united nation, coupled with a denunciation of outside interference by such powers as the IMF. In contrast, Barrios's response was cast in the colloquial style of intra-elite conversation and addressed, with ironic understatement, the all-too-familiar reality behind the embellished images constructed for outside consumption. He appealed to the elite by publically using its private language and by expressing, through self-parody that verged on self-denial, its unflattering view of Venezuela.

The Ongoing Conquest: Civilized Generals Against Primitive Masses

This view of Venezuela comes across vividly in Barrios's discussion of the country's relations with the International Monetary Fund. Barrios chooses to open this discussion by attacking Caldera for presenting himself as a nationalist leader who, unlike others, would not leave Venezuela even if the IMF policy package failed to achieve its aims. Barrios sarcastically congratulates Caldera, but declares his certainty that other respectable people, including himself, would not abandon the ship even if it threatened to sink. He then proceeds to counter Caldera's condemnation of the IMF by matter-of-factly noting that it is just a capitalist institution whose business it is to serve the interests of capitalism. He describes the IMF in terms targeted at the elite, not the masses, calling it 'a tremendously nasty, disagreeable institution [una institution tremendamente antipática, muy desagradable] whose purpose is not simply to help bankrupt nations' (Barrios 1989: 146), contrasting it with the Red Cross, whose objective is to assist countries with specific problems. The IMF's resources, Barrios emphasizes, are intended to promote capitalism, not 'to finance the corruption, waste, and administrative vices of developing nations,' adding that it would be perhaps be possible to follow Caldera and protest against the IMF's requirement that we behave in ways contrary to our own culture. However, he continues, 'I don't think we have the right to tell the IMF: "My culture of a tropical, underdeveloped country requires a certain guachafita [disorder, mess] in public administration"' (Ibid.: 147).

Barrios then gives substance to this image of a 'tropical, under-developed country' by listing a set of features which paint a negative picture of Venezuela and its elite: individual, group, and class favorit-ism; wasted public resources; poorly invested public funds, and so on. He then ends this discussion of Venezuela's relationship to the IMF on a note of sarcasm: 'It would be nice if there were an international institution with enough funds to help those who commit crimes in this fashion . . . but such an institution does not exist. As I said before, the International Red Cross serves other purposes and does not have the resources for these causes' (Ibid.).

Throughout this speech, Barrios avoids the elevated rhetoric of grand transformations, choosing instead to use the elite's private language of mundane complicity in order to elicit support for the government's program, which he defines simply as making Venezuela a 'modern state.' By adopting these (IMF-mandated) measures, Barrios argues, Venezuela would get the resources it needs and would learn to behave as a well-organized country in the future. There is no talk here of great transformations.

Noting that no one has come up with a workable alternative to the government's policies, Barrios argues that the only other possibility is to go backwards, concluding his speech by dismissing this alternative and by justifying state violence against the popular sectors with a story that 'captivated' him because of its 'implicit irony.' The anecdote concerns a British general who wanting to subdue one of the 'less primitive tribes' of Africa, sent as his emissary a missionary who had lived among the indigenous people, in the hope that he would convince them of the benefits of British occupation. The missionary told them of the hospitals, schools, means of communication and laws they would receive from the British. The African chief recognized the value of this offer, but rejected it, arguing that its acceptance would cause his people to lose their soul. On reporting the chief's refusal to the general, the missionary suggested that the chief was right. 'The general,' Barrios says, 'naturally paid no attention to the missionary and gave orders to blast the natives with heavy gunfire [plomo cerrado], as often occurs in disputes among civilized nations.' Barrios then adds, in a tone of ironic understatement, that if the congress decides to reject President Pérez's austerity program and the repressive measures taken to enforce it, the nation will begin a backward slide. 'I think that Venezuela would not necessarily return to loincloths and arrows because we have well – grounded structures and [have made] progress, but we could go back to a situation in which Rolls Royces and fancy televisions with satellite dishes would disappear' (Ibid.: 148).

The Poetics of Neocolonialism

Barrios unabashedly legitimates the new policies by passing off an old colonial framework as his own, transmuting the Venezuelan people into a 'primitive' African tribe, converting congressmen into civilizing British generals and reformulating state violence against the people as a tool of civilization. Given the Venezuelan elite's view of England as the crucible of Western capitalism, and of Africa as the dark land of primitivism, the brand of colonialism conjured up in Barrios's speech establishes a stark contrast between civilization and barbarism in which the ambiguities associated with the Spanish imperial experience in America are elided. By choosing this remote, paradigmatic colonial model, Barrios offers the local political elite an image of itself as an agent of civilization. Within the simplistic terms of this idealized model, violence against 'the primitive' can be articulated in elite-coded language, without sentimentality or grandiosity, as a necessary condition of historical progress. *Plomo cerrado* (approximately: 'heavy gunfire'), with its colloquial, laconic overtones, mimics the language of violence on the streets; it forecloses discussion.

In this speech, the conflict between barbarism to civilization is expressed through four emblematic objects. 'Loincloths and arrows' bring to mind the figure of a primitive order that lies not too far in the past and that manifests itself in the present through the Venezuelan 'Indian,' who is widely regarded as ignorant. Saved from this backward world by the existence of 'well-grounded structures' and 'progress,' the desired realm of superior civilization is conjured up by two commodities that ironically represent what is well beyond even the elite. A 'Rolls Royce,' given high domestic taxes and limited service, is a vehicle that is out of reach for most members of the upper class. As an emblem of unattainable luxury for an elite which prides itself on being able to purchase and surround itself with such external tokens of 'civilization,' it is a reminder of a distance from the metropolitan centers that not even money can entirely bridge.'Fancy televisions with satellite dishes,' on the other hand, are available to relatively large segments of the upper middle class (particularly since one satellite dish can serve many apartments in a high – rise), but access to them only emphasizes the contrast between Venezuelan and US television programs and the different societies they reflect. For those who have access to US television shows, they are a daily reminder of the gap between the two worlds, as well as a means of partially closing it; they mark both the connection and the separation between these worlds. Since from the second day of rioting Venezuelan television stations were not allowed to show what was occurring in the streets, it was through these 'fancy televisions' that the elite, including Barrios, found itself in the odd position of watching Venezuela being watched by foreign journalists and public, as the international news showed 'the horror, the primitive, the uncontrollable, from a civilized point of view, of the looting that took place in Caracas.'

Thus, through the language of objects and commodities, Barrios conjures up the image of a country suspended in an endless middle passage, eternally stranded in a transition between the threat of encroaching backwardness and the vision of receding modernity. Since he is speaking to his fellow political leaders, not to the masses, Barrios can acknowledge the limited nature of the state's goals. It is no longer a case, as with other opportunities, of proposing to take great strides towards 'modernity,' but of simply putting one's house in order, of making this 'tropical capitalism' less corrupt so as to give these politicians and the economic elite linked to them continued access to the worldly goods of the metropolitan centers. The price this ruling stratum must pay is giving up a model of protectionism that is no longer viable. But abandoning protectionism entails a violent rupture of identities which Barrios's distancing allegory cannot completely conceal. His colonial story does violence not only to the representation of the popular sectors, who must abruptly be seen as a disposable primitive mass, but also to that of the governing elite itself, to its self-image as the anti-imperialist defender of the interests of the pueblo and as the builder of Venezuelan democracy. Suddenly this political group, with its long populist and nationalist history, finds itself cast in the role of an imperial general. Minister Izaguirre's speechlessness reveals the conflicting identities the elite must negotiate in taking up this role.

With the adoption of free market policies and a shift of profit-making opportunities from local to international markets, the social and political elite increasingly has had to identify with its international counterparts and to sever its links with the popular sectors. The official image of the people as the virtuous foundation of democracy in need of tutelary guidance, has given way to a revised conception of them as backward masses in need of control. The formation of this emergent social landscape has fractured the customary bonds tying state to citizens, parties to people, and leaders to masses.

Barrios's colonial allegory must be understood within the context of a society in which political speech serves the ongoing construction of public images that conceal relations of power through the artful interplay of irony and deceit, simulation and artifice. The attention paid by Barrios to Venezuela's external image is not narcissistic but strategic: it is from the standpoint of 'civilization,' whose source lies abroad, that backwardness is constructed and that the local elite constitutes itself as a mediator between these states. In Venezuela, the political elite remains situated in an unstable neocolonial landscape which continually undermines national sources of identity and knowledge. This instability is articulated through a 'double discourse' of national identity that 'expresses and organizes the split between the appearance of national sovereignty and the continuing hold of inter-national subordination, a split inscribed in the truncated character of domestic productive relations as well as in the mimetic form of consumption values, in the production of political knowledge as well as in the formation of collective identities' (Skurski and Coronil 1993: 25).

Enunciating a Locus of Enunciation

As this brief discussion suggests, the transformation in Venezuela's social anatomy has entailed a crisis of representation which inevitably is also a crisis of self-representation. The shift from protectionist to free-market policies in Venezuela has been a violent process, with the state demonizing the popular sectors and repressing their political activism. The growing dissonance between the discourse of traditional populist nationalism and the emergent free-market discourse of eco-nomic globalization, has made shaky ground of the terrain on which social actors must now stand. The state, the locus of authoritative public speech, has been caught off balance in this ideological struggle among conflicting positions. If Izaguirre's speechlessness speaks of the state's state of crisis and offers a glimpse of a moment when history appears to hang suspended in mid-air, Barrios's speech speaks of the state's solution to the crisis and suggests its power to draw the terrain on which history must continue to unfold. In the course of mutating and mutilating the identities of both the people and their representa-tives, Barrios included, his speech shapes the contours of Venezuela's emerging neocolonial landscape. In the fault lines of this landscape we may recognize a common ground on which variously positioned subaltern subjects – and I would include here the agents of the neocolonial state in certain relational contexts – must now stand and speak.

This ground, however, should not be seen as a place beyond agency and consciousness, but as their historical product. If, as Nicos Poulantzas (1978: 114) suggests, national unity involves the 'historicity of a territory and the territorialization of a history,' then the new social geography emerging in Venezuela is a new social anatomy as well. Treating space and time as mutually constitutive dimensions of social reality may permit us to see both how postcolonial topographies are historically formed or reformed through human agency and how these spatial forms are *informed* by the meanings attached to this agency. Such a space/time perspective should also help us get beyond the analytical dichotomies that often rupture the complex unity of social life; thus, the oppositions that Spivak posits between subject position and voice, space and consciousness, may be usefully reconceptualized as relationships rather than polarized options, thereby avoiding the need to choose between them in our analyses.[6]

The locus of enunciation is inseparable from the enunciation of a locus; analysis must comprehend location and voice as interrelated dimensions of a single historical process. A subject position, therefore, is not only a locus of enunciation, but a topos partially defined by a positioned subject through speech, which in turn makes speech possible. At the height of the Venezuelan crisis, when a complex set of international and domestic forces shifted the ground on which all social actors stood, a new terrain was mapped not only by these forces, but by their representation in state speech. While in the midst of the crisis Minister Izaguirre lost his voice as well as his footing, Senator Barrios staked his claim on this new terrain by enunciating the emerging locus of state speech. Although I sympathize with Spivak's efforts to counter the conceit that intellectuals can directly represent subaltern voices or consciousness, I believe that reducing the analysis of subalternity to charting muted subject positions continues a history of silencing. Engaging with subaltern subjects entails responding to their presence within silenced histories, listening for voices – and to silences – within the cracks of dominant histories, if only to widen them.

Acknowledgements

This article is based on research supported by the Spencer Foundation and the Rackham School of Graduate Studies, University of Michigan. My gratitude to these institutions and to Julie Skurski, who has participated in every aspect of this research; to Rebecca Scott, who encouraged. me to clarify my discussion of the subaltern subject; and to my students at the University of Michigan, whose insights have deepened my understanding of these issues. All translations are mine.

[6] For fuller attempts to develop in this direction the implications of Poulantzas's insight into the interplay between geography and history, see Coronil (1996 and 1997).

Works Cited

Barrios, Gonzalo, 1989. Untitled speech, *Diario de Debates del Senado, Republica de Venezuela*, XIX (January–June 1989)1, 143–48, Caracas: Imprenta del Congreso de la Republica.

Caldera, Rafael, 1989. Untitled speech, *Diario de Debates del Senado, Republica de Venezuela*, XIX (January–June 1989)1, 135–40, Caracas: Imprenta del Congreso de la Republica.

Coronil, Fernando, 1996. 'Beyond Occidentalism: Towards Nonimperial Geohistorical Categories,' *Cultural Anthrology* 11(1), 51–87.

——, 1997. *The Magical State: Nature, Money, and Modernity in Venezuela*, Chicago: University of Chicago Press.

Coronil, Fernando, and Julie Skurski, 1991. 'Dismembering and Remembering the Nation: The Semantics of Political Violence in Venezuela,' *Comparative Studies in Society and History* 33(2), 288–337.

Hershatter, Gail, 1993. 'The Subaltern Talks Back: Reflections on Subaltern Theory and Chinese History,' *Positions* 1(1), 103–30.

Lowe, Donald, Michael Rosenthal, and Ron Silliman, 1990. 'Introduction,' 'Gayatri Spivak on the Politics of the Subaltern' (an interview with Howard Winant), *Socialist Review* 3, 81–97.

Mignolo, Walter, 1989. 'Afterword: From Colonial Discourse to Colonial Semiosis,' *Dispositio* 14, 36–8.

——, *A Darker Side of the Renaissance: Literacy, Territoriality and Colonization*, Ann Arbor: University of Michigan Press.

Parry, Benita, 1987. 'Problems in Current Theories of Colonial Discourse,' *Oxford Literary Review* 9, 27–58.

Poulantzas, Nicos, 1978. *Power, State, Socialism*, London: New Left Books.

Skurski, Julie, and Fernando Coronil, 1993. 'Country and City in a Colonial Landscape: Double Discourse and the Geopolitics of Truth in Latin America,' in *View from the Border: Essays in Honor of Raymond Williams*, ed. Dennis Dworkin and Leslie Roman, New York: Routledge, 231–59.

Spivak, Gayatri Chakravorty, 1988a. 'Can the Subaltern Speak?' in *Marxism and the Interpretation of Culture*, ed. Cary Nelson and Lawrence Grossberg, Urbana: University of Illinois Press, 271–313.

——, 1988b. 'Subaltern Studies: Deconstructing Historiography,' in *Selected Subaltern Studies*, ed. Ranajit Guha and Gayatri Chakravorty Spivak, New York: Oxford University Press, 3–32.

——, 1989. 'Naming Gayatri Spivak' (an interview with Maria Koundoura), *Stanford Humanities Review* 1, 84–97.

——, 1990. 'Qayatri Spivak on the Politics of the Subaltern' (an interview with Howard Winant), *Socialist Review* 3, 81–97.

Walton, John, 1989. 'Debt, Protest, and the State in Latin America,' in *Power and Popular Protest*, ed. Susan Eckstein, Berkeley: University of California Press, 299–328.

Young, Robert, 1990. *White Mythologies: Writing History and the West*, New York: Routledge.

Remembering Fanon, Decolonizing Diaspora

GAUTAM PREMNATH

THIS ESSAY'S TITLE is a backhanded appropriation of one of Homi Bhabha's most striking formulations. Bhabha describes his own engagement with the thought of Frantz Fanon as '*a painful re-membering*, a putting together of the dismembered past to make sense of the trauma of the present' (1994: 63; my emphasis). The sustained critique of his appropriation of Fanon in the pages that follow should not diminish the attractiveness of this statement. To dismiss Bhabha's 're-membering' as a hatchet job, as a disservice to the authentic meaning of Fanon's writings in their moment, is pointless.[1] We cannot reconstitute the New Man of the 1960s, nor should we try; to turn the task of elaborating Fanon's provocative body of writings into a contest over who gets to bear away the body of the dead hero is a narcissistic exercise and an intellectual dead-end. The question is rather one of ethical decision. From the standpoint of diaspora, how do we choose to re-member Fanon? Which Fanon do we choose to re-member?

The appearance of *Nation and Narration* (Bhabha 1990) is something of a landmark moment in recent humanistic scholarship. In their articulation of the historiography of nationalism with the theory of narrative, and especially in their soundings of correspondences between the nation-form and the genre of the novel, this collection of essays is a marker of the transformation of an emergent mode of inquiry into one of the most widespread thematic concerns of contemporary literary studies.[2] Many of the essays also bear out the claim that closes Eric Hobsbawm's monograph on nationalism of the same year: 'the owl of Minerva which brings wisdom, said Hegel, only flies out at dusk. It is a good sign that it is now circling round nations and nationalism' (1990: 192). Hobsbawm's comment identifies the theoretical bivalence of

---

[1] I note this tendency in the otherwise salutary critique of postcolonialist readings of Fanon in Robinson 1993.

[2] Of course equally if not more significant in this regard is Benedict Anderson's *Imagined Communities* (1983), a work whose influence is palpable throughout *Nation and Narration*.

much contemporary scholarship on nationalism: its retrospective gaze also has a prospective vocation. The study of nationalism is often the point of departure for attempts to understand new transnational logics that are rapidly outflanking the system of nation-states.

Significantly, the rise to prominence of such scholarly pursuits has coincided with an ongoing revival of interest in the thought of Frantz Fanon in the Anglo-American academy, a revival that as yet shows no signs of abating. Indeed, in his editor's introduction to *Nation and Narration*, Homi Bhabha claims that the volume as a whole 'seeks to affirm and extend Fanon's revolutionary credo: "National consciousness, which is not nationalism, is the only thing that will give us an international dimension."' Bhabha continues:

> It is this *inter*national dimension both within the margins of the nation-space and in the boundaries *in-between* nations and peoples that the authors of this book have sought to represent in their essays. The representative emblem of this book might be a chiasmatic 'figure' of cultural difference whereby the anti-nationalist, ambivalent nation-space becomes the crossroads to a new transnational culture. (Bhabha 1990: 4)

I share with Bhabha the belief that Fanon's work can powerfully inform theoretical figurations of transnational culture. This belief is grounded in a reading of *The Wretched of the Earth* that recognizes that for Fanon 'national consciousness' does not reconstitute a primordial community. Thus Fanonian national consciousness evades the misadventures of Volkisch and territorial nationalism, rendering it eminently appropriable for a transnational politics. For the purposes of such a movement beyond anti-colonial nationalism, Bhabha's formulations seem thus far unexceptionable. Yet I want to return to his elaboration upon Fanon's 'revolutionary credo' to consider some of its implications for our understanding of transnational culture. Two aspects in particular bear careful consideration:

(1) the gloss of Fanon's words that collapses the careful formulation 'national consciousness, which is not nationalism' into the simple 'anti-nationalist.'
(2) the reinscription of the gridwork of the system of nation-states, such that 'the new transnational culture' emerges out of its interstices. Thus processes of globalization are themselves assimilated to a discourse of interstitiality and marginality. This renders illegible the transnational culture of Coca-Cola, Shell Oil, and the Hinduja

family – that is to say, a 'transnational corporatism' that overrides, rather than negotiates within, the grid of state–state relations.[3]

These are important moments in Bhabha's reading of Fanon. They combine to diminish the project of decolonization that animated Fanon's intellectual production, while simultaneously failing to register the economic and geopolitical transformations that have made it necessary to move this project beyond the horizon of nation-based anti-colonialism for a transnational emancipatory politics. Working from the premise that decolonization is an incomplete rather than superseded project, I wish to argue for a different relationship to the history of anti-colonial nationalism, one that can retrieve its traditions of resistance for the contestation of new forms of imperialism.

Another Bhabha essay, 'DissemiNation' (originally published as part of *Nation and Narration*), closes with a discussion of the phantasmatic metropolis *Ellowen Deeowen*/London in Salman Rushdie's *The Satanic Verses*, of which he claims, 'it is to the city that the migrants, the minorities, the diasporic come to change the history of the nation' (Bhabha 1994: 169–70). Here the migrant in the metropolis serves as the authorizing sign for Bhabha's joint devaluing of anti-colonial and imperial nationalism. This is one illustration of how, within the field of postcolonial studies, the increasing salience of discourses of migrancy and diaspora has often worked to disconnect postcolonialist intellectual production from the vicissitudes of the formally independent, formerly-colonized nation-state. Arjun Appadurai, for instance, presents the diasporic construction of the Sikh homeland of Khalistan as evidence of a 'new, postnational cartography.' He argues that 'the topos of Sikh "national" identity is in fact a topos of "community" (*qom*), which contests many national maps. . . and contains one model of a post-Westphalian cartography' (Appadurai 1996: 50).[4] Such an assertion passes blithely over the structuring of the discourse of Khalistan by the activities of the Indian state, ranging from the political machinations in the 1970s of Indira Gandhi's Congress (I) Party (at that point still the de facto organ of authoritarian state centralism in India) to the police and military campaigns of the 1980s and 1990s.[5] The haste to demarcate and occupy the space of the 'postnational,' a move heavily informed by Bhabha's influential criticism, affords few critical tools

---

[3] I take the phrase 'transnational corporatism' from Miyoshi 1993.
[4] Elsewhere in the same article Appadurai locates the Westphalian treaties of 1648 as the moment when 'territorial sovereignty becomes the foundational concept of the nation-state' (41).

with which to address this ongoing reality of the interventionist nation-state.[6]

Thus the postcolonialist concern with diaspora all too often signals a departure from what Edward Said calls 'secular criticism.' Said's definition of the critic's situation – 'to stand between culture and system is therefore to stand close to . . . a concrete reality about which political, moral, and social judgments have to be made and, if not only made, then exposed and demystified' (Said 1983: 26) – implies an oppositional relationship, 'within and against' national formations such as the university, the newspaper, and the ministry of culture.[7] Such an intellectual politics recognizes that the nation-state continues to constitute the horizon of day-to-day experience for much of the world's population under conditions of neo-colonialism, perhaps especially as the conduit through which the violence of globalization is visited upon its subject people. Yet Said's formulation implies a non-absolutist conception of the state – a sense that it is amenable to transformative action. Such an understanding is far from the 'common sense' in contemporary postcolonial studies. Instead the field is characterized by doctrinaire assertions that the goal of historical decolonization was no more and no less than the modernization of a colonized people via the imposition of intractable state structures.[8] Increasingly, these are coupled with claims that globalization does not refunction these structures but rather renders them irrelevant.[9]

In such an intellectual context, the problematic of diaspora allows

[5] For a treatment of the discourse of Khalistan that continually brings forth evidence of the ubiquity within it of the Indian state, see Mahmood 1996.
[6] Witness, in contrast, the prophesy of Senegal-based political economist Samir Amin. Amin describes how 'the growing interpenetration of national systems of production . . . cancels out the effectiveness of traditional national policies and delivers the system as a whole up to the command – and transgressions of world market pressures alone.' Yet he tempers this (now quite well-established) account of globalization with the prediction 'that the "national factor" is far from having been neutralized by the trends which globalization will force on the economic system, and that it is . . . on the road to trying to prevail once more over the very logic of economic development' (Amin 1996, 33–4). See also Patnaik 1995.
[7] On the critic's relation to the state, see Said 1983, 11.
[8] The invariable point of reference for these claims is Chatterjee 1986. For a more modest argument, grounded in the political economy of Haiti, see Trouillot 1990.
[9] For a recent critique of such an embrace of globalization by anti-statist thinkers in India such as Gail Omvedt, in the context of debates over the political economy of caste and class, see Ilaiah 1997 and Natrajan et al., 1998.

for movement beyond what seems like a parochial and dated location, and an entry to the space of global citizenship.[10] The title of a recent work of criticism by R. Radhakrishnan, *Diasporic Mediations*, expresses this determinant of diasporic intellectualism very well. In a gloss of his title, Radhakrishnan defines diasporic location as 'the space of the hyphen that tries to coordinate, within an evolving relationship, the identity politics of one's place of origin with that of one's present home . . . with my diasporic displacement there is a "now" and a "then" to my life, underwritten by a "here" and a "there"' (1996: xiii–xiv). Radhakrishnan is careful to frame this account of spatio-temporal dislocation in exclusively autobiographical terms, describing an individual's willed movement from his birthplace in India to his current position as a professor in an American university. Yet in counterposing the 'here and now' of metropolitan contemporaneity to the 'there and then' of his place of origin in the Third World, this life-story reads as a self-serving parable of cosmopolitanism. In the process, it reinscribes the 'denial of coevalness' of metropolis and periphery that Johannes Fabian has identified as one of the classic orienting devices of historical imperialism (1983). Moreover, in presenting diasporic displacement as the enabling condition for his considerations of postcoloniality, Radhakrishnan refuses the politics of location that Said elaborates for the secular critic, an oppositional stance 'close to the concrete reality' of the postcolonial or neo-imperial nation-state.[11] Yet, as his essay on 'effective' intellectualism (Radhakrishnan 1996: 27–61) demonstrates especially clearly, much of his thinking is informed by political shifts that are specific to a US–American context, and that bespeak transformations in the state–civil society relationship in the USA during the epoch of Reagan.

Such a realization can help us to locate the 'here and now' of Bhabha's meditations on nationalism and identity. My sense is that Bhabha's influential writings of the 1980s are 'grounded' in the shifting political terrain of Thatcherite Britain, and are in large measure shaped in response to the consolidation of the political project of Thatcherism during that decade. Margaret Thatcher, of course, is famous for claiming (after Hayek) that 'there is no such thing as society.'[12] Instead

---

[10] On this point my position is similar to those taken by Aijaz Ahmad in his recent writings. See especially Ahmad 1992.

[11] I should clarify that I do not take Said's formulation to imply *geographical* proximity.

[12] In a 1987 interview with the British magazine *Woman's Own*, quoted in Thatcher 1997, 576.

she proposed a politics rhetorically grounded in the individual-as-householder, whose horizontal identifications with like individuals constitute the imagined community of the nation. Thatcherism's success as a political project lay in large measure in its generation of a discourse of national belonging that could both systematically obliterate the consciousness of social processes and structurings and serve as symbolic compensation for the aggressive dismantling of the postwar welfarist consensus. Thus an ideology of national community underwrote Thatcherism's 'anti-statist' statism, effecting a radical transformation of British society even as Margaret Thatcher herself loudly denied the very existence of such a thing as British *society*.[13]

This majoritarian discourse of national community requires the racially minor figure as its point of closure. The role race plays here is not 'arbitrary' – this figure is necessarily racialized, not for some transhistorical reason, but because of the historical fusing of racial and national identity under the aegis of the late and post-imperial British state.[14] Yet this form of majoritarian statism also generates minoritarian counterparts. Commenting on the response of some Bradford South Asian Muslims to Salman Rushdie's *The Satanic Verses*, Gayatri Spivak argues that 'the desire of these British Muslims is not to abdicate from the nation, but to insert Islamic education into the state. To participate in the nation in general, and yet to remain an enclave' (1994: 236). Thus two discourses of community – majoritarian and minoritarian, xenophobic and 'ethnic' – form two sides of the same statist coin. Yet as state sovereignty fades under the imperatives of globalization, the heretofore interminable circuit between these two discourses of community increasingly undergoes interference and interruption. Out of the sputterings of this circuit emerge new understandings of sovereignty and agency, no longer guaranteed by a seemingly all-powerful state.

It is in this context that Bhabha's theory of hybridity has been able to acquire its remarkable critical purchase. In a recent article Bhabha has provided a description of what is at stake in his use of this term:

> In my own work I have developed the concept of hybridity to describe the construction of cultural authority within conditions of political antagonism or inequity. . . . the hybrid strategy or discourse opens up a space of negotiation where power is *unequal* but its

---

[13] For a compelling account of the 'imposture' of Thatcherite animosity towards state power, see Elliott 1993, 96–7.
[14] The best argument for this is to be found in Tabili 1994. On this point, if not others, I also find common ground with Smith 1994.

articulation may be *equivocal*. Such negotiation is neither assimilation nor collaboration. It makes possible the emergence of an
'interstitial' agency that refuses the binary representation of social
antagonism. (Bhabha 1993: 212)

In essays such as 'Interrogating Identity' this interstitial agency is
invested in the figure of the (Third World) migrant in the (First
World) metropolis, and emerges from in-between the post-imperial
xenophobia of 'Little England' and the vanguardist elitism of Third
World nationalist leaders (Bhabha 1994: 40–65). Yet such an analysis,
by virtue of its parasitical relationship to the very antagonism it stages,[15]
cannot address the supersession of both Little England and nation-based
decolonization by a new global logic – represented in one case by the
imperative to dissolve national specificity into a single European market;
and in the other by structural adjustment programs that demand the
signing over of state sovereignty to the World Bank/IMF combine.

This realization should give us pause as we consider Bhabha's
advocacy of a politics of negotiation. It is important to remember
that the very language of 'negotiation' emerges in British cultural
studies to name a mode of engagement with 'dominant culture.'[16] The
decisive impact of this concept, in work such as Stuart Hall's early
essays on media practice, is to call attention to the hegemonic
processes by means of which dominance is reproduced. Yet the concept
of negotiation always operates here in tandem with that of the
oppositional. Thus Hall concludes the essay entitled 'Encoding/Decod-
ing' by discussing how 'the struggle in discourse' is joined in moments
when the dominant is in crisis, and 'events which are normally signified
and decoded in a negotiated way begin to be given an oppositional
reading' (1980: 138). Yet since the 1970s this theoretical emphasis on
oppositionality has increasingly been displaced, in Hall's own work as
well as in the growing body of work informed by his influential
writings.[17] In a recent essay Hall assimilates even traditions of

[15] In using the term 'parasitical' I have in mind Rey Chow's recent advocacy of
a cultural politics based on the premise that 'it is necessary to think *primarily* in
terms of borders – of borders, that is, as *para-sites* that never take over a field but
erode it slowly and *tactically*' (1993: 16; Chow's emphasis).
[16] I draw here upon the account offered by Alan Sinfield of the formulation of
the troika of dominant–negotiated–oppositional in the work of sociologist
Frank Parkin, and its taking up by Raymond Williams and Stuart Hall, among
others (Sinfield 1994: 66–7).
[17] For some examples, see Hall 1986, Hall 1995, and Mercer 1994. For another
line out of Hall see my discussion of Paul Gilroy below.

marronage and autonomous community (such as Rastafari) to the idea of cultural negotiation.[18] The oppositional moment seems to take place at some ever-receding horizon, even as the language of crisis has become ubiquitous in contemporary cultural studies.

A related development can be traced in Bhabha's essay 'The Commitment to Theory,' written in response to the perceived anti-theoretical excesses of a rhapsodic third world-ism. This essay, despite its ostensibly anti-programmatic impulse, gives the theoretical principle of cultural hybridity and its accompanying strategy of cultural negotiation something like a programmatic formulation. Bhabha voices his commitment in polemical response to what he sees as the anti-theoretical organizational imperative of actually-existing socialism:

> Too often these theoretical issues are peremptorily transposed into organisational terms and represented as 'sectarianism.' I am suggesting that such contradictions and conflicts, which often thwart political intentions and make the question of commitment complex and difficult, are rooted in the process of translation and displacement in which the 'object' of politics is inscribed. The effect is . . . the spur to the 'negotiation' of socialist democratic politics and policies which demand that questions of organisation are theorised and socialist theory is 'organised,' *because there is no given community or body of the people whose inherent, radical historicity emits the right signs.* (Bhabha 1994: 26–7; Bhabha's emphasis)

Bhabha suggests that the demand for 'organisation' is compelled by anxiety over the inadequacy or belatedness of a properly self-identical subject-object of politics ('the people'), which must hence be 'organised' into existence. As an alternative to such a top-down imposition of organizational form upon the cultural field, he proposes a practice of cultural negotiation. His articulation of this practice is couched in a remarkable appropriation of Fanon. Commenting in the same essay on *The Wretched of the Earth* he claims:

> In the moment of liberatory struggle, the Algerian people destroy the continuities and constancies of the 'nationalist' tradition which provided a safeguard against colonial cultural imposition. *They are now free to negotiate and translate their cultural identities in a discontinuous intertextual temporality of cultural difference.* (Bhabha 1994: 38; my emphasis)

---

[18] For a discussion of a similar tendency in Bhabha's work, see Parry 1994, 8.

'Struggle' functions here primarily as a theoretical occasion for the principle of negotiation, seemingly bereft of any relationship to organized movement. This positing of a numinous moment of struggle serves to mystify the processual unfolding of decolonization. Thus it erases the dialogic interplay between nationalism (here rigidified as ' "nationalist" tradition') and national consciousness that is at the heart of Fanon's theoretical endeavours in *The Wretched of the Earth*. In the passage Bhabha is glossing, one of the best-known in *Wretched*, Fanon goes on to proclaim: 'it is to this zone of occult instability where the people dwell that we must come' (Fanon 1966: 182). While Bhabha often returns to this striking statement, he continually de-emphasizes its status, in Fanon's text, as an injunction to nationalist *intellectuals*. In relentlessly reinscribing nationalism as bad object, his 're-membering' must *forget* the crucial imperative of nationalist organization and intellectual direction in Fanon's writing.

My reminder of this aspect of Fanon's thought should not be construed as a revanchist response to Bhabha's critique of the demand for 'organisation.' Rather, I want to call attention to Fanon's very different framing of the problem posed by top-down leadership. Bhabha's problematization of political leadership relies on mapping the distinction between nationalism and national consciousness onto a rigid conceptual split between the *pedagogical*, marked by a 'continuist, accumulative temporality' and the *performative*, characterized by a 'repetitious, recursive strategy' (Bhabha 1994: 145). Having established this rigid binary, he then emphasizes the aleatory possibilities emerging out of the ambivalent space in-between. In contrast, Fanon's essay 'Spontaneity: Its Strength and Weakness' in *The Wretched of the Earth* begins by identifying 'a time-lag, or difference of rhythm, between the leaders of a nationalist party and the mass of the people' (Fanon 1966: 87).[19] By posing the problem in terms of *rhythm*, Fanon immediately gives us a more supple way of conceptualizing the time of politics than either the linear, continuist temporality Bhabha identifies with nationalist thought or the repetitious temporality he invests in the consciousness of a nation-people.

In Fanon's account the process of decolonization is a bringing into rhythm of nationalism and national consciousness. Specifically, this is instigated by the splitting off from the party of an 'illegal' nationalist tendency that affiliates itself with the mass of the people and incites

---

[19] Bhabha puts Fanon's concept of 'time-lag' to very different account in the essay ' "Race," Time, and the Revision of Modernity' (Bhabha 1994, 235–56).

rebellion. Yet, rather than spontaneous struggle, this rebellion is marked by the elaboration of a new organizational form:

> All this taking stock of the situation, this enlightening of con-sciousness and this advance in the knowledge of the history of societies are only possible within the framework of an organisation, and inside the structure of a people. Such an organisation is set afoot by the use of revolutionary elements coming from the towns at the beginning of the rising, together with those rebels who go down into the country as the fight goes on. It is this core which constitutes the embryonic political organisation of the rebellion. But on the other hand the peasants who are all the time adding to their knowledge in the light of experience, will come to show themselves capable of directing the people's struggle. Between the nation on a war-time footing and its leaders there is established a mutual current of enlightenment and enrichment. (Fanon 1966: 114)

Rather than glorifying an elite cadre of vanguardist intellectuals, leading the mass of the population to 'catch up' with it along a unilinear developmental path of revolutionary consciousness, Fanon emphasizes the 'mutual current' between leaders and people. Rather than occulting the pedagogical dimension of intellectual labor, he conceives of a mode of pedagogical leadership premised on the principle of mutual recognition being realized in the new national community, in which the roles of leaders and led are interchangeable. Thus is elaborated an organizational framework in which nationalist leadership and the activity of a nation-people continually bring each other in line – or, more precisely, in rhythm.[20]

The subtle theorist and visionary thinker of political organization – this is not, by and large, the Fanon who is remembered in the Anglo-American academy today. Even as there has been an explosion of scholarly work on his writings in recent years, its cumulative effect has been to recentre the Fanonian corpus around Black Skin, White Masks.[21] Such work tends to marginalize the complex understanding of 'national consciousness' derived from the experience of decolonizing Algeria. The narrator of 'The Fact of Blackness,' the most frequently-cited

[20] For a historical account of decolonizing nationalism which, without referen-cing Fanon, delineates a similar 'mutual current' between nationalist leadership and the activity of a nation-people, see Sarkar 1983.
[21] Hall 1996, drawing heavily on Bhabha's work, offers a spirited justification of this move. For what amounts to an impressive rebuttal, see the essays collected in Gordon et al., 1996.

chapter of *Black Skin, White Masks*, speaks as an ordinary practitioner in metropolitan space, his neurosis instigated by the refusal of the abstract universal citizenship to which he lays claim. A collectivity defined by race emerges – is 'secreted' – out of the individualized anomie of this Martiniquan *evolué* in Paris (Fanon 1967a: 122). Here the narrative of racialization coincides neatly with the narrative of modern individuation familiar to readers of Lacan in basic statements such as 'The Mirror Stage' and 'Aggressivity in Psychoanalysis' (Lacan 1977: 1–7, 8–29). This has made *Black Skin, White Masks* a convenient point of departure for Western critics interested in elaborating psychoanalytic epistemologies of race.[22] Moreover, it has in some sense worked to present the protagonist of 'The Fact of Blackness' as the quintessential subject of Fanonian discourse. Such an engagement with Fanon, in failing to pursue his intellectual trajectory beyond the provisional conclusion of *Black Skin, White Masks*, breaks off the dialectical drama of Fanon's perpetual questioning, and the manner in which his writings on Algeria respond to the dilemmas voiced in earlier writings.[23]

Consider, for instance, Kobena Mercer's claim that 'the [diasporic] interest in *Black Skin, White Masks*, in contrast to Fanon's other texts . . . could be understood as a response to the failures of revolutionary nationalism' (1996: 116).[24] The fact of these 'failures' is presented as a commonplace, uninterrogated and unexplained. Yet equally significant is that Mercer does not ask what it might mean to return to the scene of Fanon's first book as if the Algerian Revolution had never happened – that is to say, to derive a 'post-nationalist' politics from what is in many regards a *pre*-nationalist text. In contrast, Aijaz Ahmad has recently offered the following proposition about nationalism: 'you can't bypass it, you have to go *through* it, find your way to the other side of it' (1996:

---

[22] Apart from previously-cited work by Bhabha, Hall, and Mercer, I am thinking here of essays such as Doane 1991, Fuss 1995, and Lloyd 1991.

[23] I draw here upon the detailed and authoritative argument for reading Fanon's writings as a single dramatic narrative in Sekyi-Otu 1996. See also Lazarus 1993, who argues that Bhabha 'contrives to read [Fanon] "back to front" – that is from *The Wretched of the Earth* to *Black Skin, White Masks* – thereby falsifying the testimony of Fanon's own evolution as a theorist' (87).

[24] Elsewhere Mercer says, 'I would argue that one of the reasons why *Black Skin, White Masks* has been re-read with such a sense of urgency has to do with Fanon's recognition of the value of psychoanalysis as the site of the talking cure' (1996: 121). In light of this claim it is important to emphasize that Fanon's institutional critique of colonial ethnopsychiatry never led to a break from psychoanalytic method, even in his later writings. See, for instance, 'Colonial War and Mental Disorders' (Fanon 1966: 203–51).

405). In the context of the vexed relationship between First World diaspora and Third World nation, adhering to such a principle might help to identify the living legacies of anti-colonial nationalism in diasporic practice. It also helps to explain why Fanon's analysis of 'national consciousness' could and should inform the theoretical agenda for treatments of diasporic identity. Such work would connect the current concerns of diaspora studies to new horizons of decolonization, by articulating the movements of identity with the self-organization of people.[25]

Cornel West seems to gesture toward such a project on the book-jacket of a recent work of African-American cultural criticism, where he hails its author as 'a new kind of intellectual of the younger generation.' West substantiates this characterization by describing how 'she goes beyond the fashionable mantra of Race, Gender and Class by concretely situating black people constructing themselves as a community on the move geographically, culturally, politically, and existentially.'[26] Yet his comments are evidence, if anything, of the *un*fashionability of the analytical troika of race, gender, and class in contemporary academic discourse. If the theoretical practices this 'mantra' invokes have been constantly assailed from the academic (and extra-academic) right, they now seem to be losing ground on the academic left as well. Increasingly, as West's language suggests, they are being surpassed by a new discourse of *community*, characterized by a horizontality that overwrites, levels, and smoothes the stratifications and fractures named by 'Race, Gender and Class.' This has prompted a general revival of interest in this topic among cultural theorists interested in elaborating upon a bland colloquial usage that invests 'community' in any and all collocations of human beings.[27] This is in some ways a salutary development, placing the focus, as West's language also suggests, on the construction of solidaristic identifications over and above fragmented identities. Yet 'Race, Gender, and

[25] One benchmark for such work is provided by Alexander 1997, who envisions 'an emancipatory praxis anchored within a desire for decolonization, imagined simultaneously as political, economic, psychic, discursive, *and* sexual' (100).
[26] Cornel West, book-jacket testimonial for Griffin 1995.
[27] See Young 1990 and, for an account of this critical tendency of particular relevance to postcolonial studies, Dhareshwar 1995. With reference to diaspora, see Tölölyan 1991, who claims that 'diasporas are the exemplary communities of the transnational moment' (5); and the groundbreaking theorizations of diasporic community in Gilroy 1982, Gilroy 1987, and Gilroy 1993.

Class' names more than a mere string of identity-fetishes. This 'mantra' also identifies social and state logics that shape and direct the constitution of community. To see 'community' as *replacing* this analytical tool is to subscribe to a conceptually vacuous and politically emptied usage of the term.

West's deployment of community seems to bear out Cindy Patton's acute characterization of latter-day cultural studies as the replacing of a 'worn-out social with a polished-up cultural' (1993: 167). Yet an alternative model for theorizing diasporic community is available within the line of British cultural studies itself, in early essays by Paul Gilroy such as 'Steppin' Out of Babylon – Race, Class, and Autonomy' (1982). Here Gilroy argues that 'autonomous organisation has allowed blacks and women to leapfrog over their fellow workers into direct confrontation with the state in the interest of the class as a whole' (304). Diasporic black communities for Gilroy are more than negotiated responses to metropolitan dominance; they also retrieve political traditions of resistance:

> The lingering bile of slavery, indenture and colonialism remains – not in the supposedly pathological forms in which black households are organised, but in the forms of struggle, political philosophy, and revolutionary perspectives of non-European radical traditions, and the 'good sense' of their practical ideologies. (Gilroy 1982: 285–6)

Such an argument, reminiscent of A. Sivanandan's formulation of diasporic black self-organization as the constitution of 'communities of resistance' (Sivanandan 1990), puts Fanon firmly on the theoretical agenda for a diasporic politics. The crucial point here is that Fanon's understanding of colonialism will not allow for a continuist under-standing of community – an operating assumption is that there can be no recovery of the precolonial past except in pulverized, fragmentary forms. As Fanon put it in his famous address to the First Congress of Negro Writers and Artists in 1956, colonialism breaks the 'systems of reference' of the precolonial community: 'The lines of force, having crumbled, no longer give direction' (Fanon 1967b: 33). In the wake of this catastrophe, there can be no going back: 'The struggle for freedom does not give back to the national culture its former values and shapes' (Fanon 1966: 197). The massive psychic displacement of colonialism has been reworked into the substance of the national community. To the extent that traditions are retrievable, they must be retrieved as traditions *of resistance*.

In his celebrated long poem 'Turner,' the British-based Guyanese poet David Dabydeen offers a rich allegory for this process in diaspora. The poem is provoked by John Ruskin's notorious failure, in a lavish critical treatment of J.M.W. Turner's painting 'Slavers Throwing Overboard the Dead and Dying,' to more than barely notice the dead and dying subjects in the foreground of the canvas. Focusing on the submerged head of a drowned man in Turner's painting, Dabydeen fabricates a richly-realized African past for him. A key element of this imagined past is the figure of Manu, magician and keeper of secrets of the tribe.[28] In a prophetic moment, prior to the arrival of the slavers, Manu rips apart his necklace of jouti beads. The assembled children race to gather the scattered beads, 'each child clutching an accidental handful where before they hung in a sequence of hues/ Around his neck, the pattern of which only he/ Knew – from his father and those before – to preserve.' Yet when the children look to Manu for explanation, they receive only this prediction:

> That in the future each must learn to live
> Beadless in a foreign land; or perish.
> Or each must learn to make new jouti,
> Arrange them by instinct, imagination, study
> And arbitrary choice into a pattern
> Pleasing to the self and others
> Of the scattered tribe; or perish. Each
> Will be barren of ancestral memory
> But each richly endowed with such emptiness
> From which to dream, surmise, invent, immortalise.
>   (Dabydeen 1994: 33)

The drowned subject of Dabydeen's poem cannot realize this prophesy, and indeed his tortured wrestlings with the past serve to problematize the diasporic hope of beginning life anew. Yet the context of Black Britain offers rich evidence of how diasporic subjects have re-membered tradition and community in response to the dislocations – catastrophic and volitional – that constitute diaspora experience. The sureties of another social order have been scattered, yet the regathering of the fragments of the past and their reconstitution as traditions of resistance are among the most striking deployments of

---

[28] It is crucial that Dabydeen forbids the idealizing of this past by giving his imaginary African sage the same name as the legendary giver of Brahminical, patriarchal laws in ancient India.

diasporic 'emptiness.' As theory strives to stay in rhythm with these developments, 'instinct, imagination, and study' would do well to lead us back to the thought of Frantz Fanon.

Acknowledgments

For engagement, encouragement, and inspiration, I thank Kasturi Ray, Vijay Prashad, Elisabeth Armstrong, Neil Lazarus, Annette Van, Lloyd Pratt, Elisa Glick, and Benita Parry.

Works Cited

Ahmad, Aijaz, 1992. 'Salman Rushdie's *Shame*: Postmodern Migrancy and the Representation of Women,' in *In Theory: Nations, Classes, Literatures*, London: Verso, 123–258.

———, 1996. *Lineages of the Present: Political Essays*, New Delhi: Tulika.

Alexander, M. Jacqui, 1997. 'Erotic Autonomy as a Politics of Decolonization: An Analysis of Feminist and State Practice in the Bahamas Tourist Economy,' in M. Jacqui Alexander and Chandra Talpade Mohanty, eds., *Feminist Genealogies, Colonial Legacies, Democratic Futures*, London, New York: Routledge, 63–100.

Amin, Samir, 1996. 'The New Capitalist Globalization: Problems and Perspectives,' *Links* 7, 25–34.

Anderson, Benedict, 1983. *Imagined Communities: Reflections on the Origins and Spread of Nationalism*, London: Verso.

Appadurai, Arjun, 1996. 'Sovereignty without Territoriality: Notes for a Postnational Geography,' in Patricia Yaeger, ed., *The Geography of Identity*, Ann Arbor: University of Michigan Press, 40–58.

Bhabha, Homi, ed., 1990. *Nation and Narration*, London, New York: Routledge.

———, 1993. 'Culture's In Between,' *Artforum* September, 167–8, 211–12, 214.

———, 1994. *The Location of Culture*, London, New York: Routledge.

Chatterjee, Partha, 1986. *Nationalist Thought and the Colonial World: A Derivative Discourse?*, London: Zed Books.

Chow, Rey, 1993. *Writing Diaspora: Tactics of Intervention in Contemporary Cultural Studies*, Bloomington: Indiana University Press.

Dabydeen, David, 1994. *Turner: New and Selected Poems*, London: Jonathan Cape.

Dhareshwar, Vivek, 1995. '"Our Time": History, Sovereignty, and Politics,' *Economic and Political Weekly* 30(6), 317–24.

Doane, Mary Ann, 1991. 'Dark Continents: Epistemologies of Racial and Sexual Difference in Psychoanalysis and the Cinema,' in *Femmes Fatales: Feminism, Film Theory, Psychoanalysis*, New York, London: Routledge.

Elliott, Gregory, 1993. *Labourism and the English Genius: The Strange Death of Labour England?*, London: Verso.

Fabian, Johannes, 1983. *Time and the Other: How Anthropology Makes Its Object*, New York: Columbia University Press.

Fanon, Frantz, 1966. *The Wretched of the Earth*, trans. Constance Farrington, New York: Grove Press. Originally published in 1961 as *Les Damnées de la Terre*, Paris: François Maspero.

——, 1967a. *Black Skin, White Masks*, trans. Charles Lam Markmann, New York: Grove Press. Originally published in 1952 as *Peau Noire, Masques Blancs*, Paris: Editions du Seuil.

——, 1967b. *Toward the African Revolution*, trans. Haakon Chevalier, New York: Monthly Review Press. Originally published in 1964 as *Pour la Révolution Africaine*, Paris: François Maspero.

Fuss, Diana, 1995. 'Interior Colonies: Frantz Fanon and the Politics of Identification,' in *Identification Papers*, London, New York: Routledge, 141–72.

Gilroy, Paul, 1982. 'Steppin' out of Babylon: Race, Class, and Autonomy,' in Centre for Contemporary Cultural Studies, *The Empire Strikes Back: Race and Racism in 70s Britain*, London: Hutchinson, 276–314.

——, 1987. *'There Ain't No Black in the Union Jack': The Cultural Politics of Race and Nation*, London: Hutchinson.

——, 1993. *The Black Atlantic: Modernity and Double-Consciousness*, Cambridge: Harvard University Press.

Gordon, Lewis, T. Denean Sharpley-Whiting, and Renée White, 1996. *Fanon: A Critical Reader*, Oxford: Blackwell.

Griffin, Farah Jasmine, 1995. *'Who Set You Flowin'?': The African-American Migration Narrative*, New York: Oxford University Press.

Hall, Stuart, 1980. 'Encoding/Decoding,' in Centre for Contemporary Cultural Studies, *Culture, Media, Language: Working Papers in Cultural Studies, 1972–79*, London: Hutchinson, 128–38.

——, 1986. 'Minimal Selves,' in Lisa Appignanesi, *The Real Me: Post-Modernism and the Question of Identity*, ICA Documents 6, London: ICA, 44–6.

——, 1995. 'Negotiating Caribbean Identities,' *New Left Review* 209, 3–14.

——, 1996. 'The After-life of Frantz Fanon: Why Fanon? Why Now? Why *Black Skin, White Masks*?' in Alan Read, ed., *The Fact of Blackness: Frantz Fanon and Visual Representation*, London: ICA, 12–37.

Hobsbawm, Eric, 1990. *Nations and Nationalism since 1780: Programme, Myth, Reality*, Cambridge: Cambridge University Press.

Ilaiah, Kancha, 1997. 'Dalits and Globalization,' *The Hindu*, 11 November, 12.

Lacan, Jacques, 1977. *Écrits: A Selection*, trans. Alan Sheridan, New York: W.W. Norton.

Lazarus, Neil, 1993. 'Disavowing Decolonization: Fanon, Nationalism, and the Problematic of Representation in Current Theories of Colonial Discourse,' *Research in African Literatures* 24(4), 69–98.

Lloyd, David, 1991. 'Race under Representation,' *Oxford Literary Review* 13 (1–2), 62–94.

Mahmood, Cynthia Keppley, 1996. *Fighting for Faith and Nation: Dialogues with Sikh Militants*, Philadelphia: University of Pennsylvania Press.

Mercer, Kobena, 1994. *Welcome to the Jungle: New Positions in Black Cultural Studies*, London, New York: Routledge.

———, 1996. 'Decolonisation and Disappointment: Reading Fanon's Sexual Politics,' in Alan Read, ed., *The Fact of Blackness: Frantz Fanon and Visual Representation*, London: ICA, 114–31.

Miyoshi, Masao, 1993. 'A Borderless World? From Colonialism to Transnationalism and the Decline of the Nation-State,' *Critical Inquiry* 19(4), 726–51.

Natrajan, Balmurli, Ciarán ó Faoláin, and Kavita Philip, 1998. 'SAPs, Dust, and Hot Air: Gail Omvedt and Liberalization,' *Ghadar* 2(1), 1 and 6–10.

Parry, Benita, 1994. 'Signs of Our Times,' *Third Text* 28/29, 5–24.

Patnaik, Prabhat, 1995. 'A Note on the Political Economy of the "Retreat of the State",' in *Whatever Happened to Imperialism and Other Essays*, New Delhi: Tulika, 194–210.

Patton, Cindy, 1993. 'Tremble, Hetero Swine!' in Michael Warner, ed., *Fear of a Queer Planet: Queer Politics and Social Theory*, Minneapolis: University of Minnesota Press, 143–77.

Radhakrishnan, R., 1996. *Diasporic Mediations: Between Home and Location*, Minneapolis: University of Minnesota Press.

Robinson, Cedric, 1993. 'The Appropriation of Frantz Fanon,' *Race and Class* 35 (1), 79–91.

Said, Edward, 1983. *The World, the Text, and the Critic*, Cambridge: Harvard University Press.

Sarkar, Sumit, 1983. *Modern India: 1885–1947*, New Delhi: Macmillan.

Sekyi-Otu, Ato, 1996. *Fanon's Dialectic of Experience*, Cambridge: Harvard University Press.

Sinfield, Alan, 1994. *Cultural Politics – Queer Reading*, Philadelphia: University of Pennsylvania Press.

Sivanandan, A., 1990. *Communities of Resistance: Writings on Black Struggles for Socialism*, London: Verso.

Smith, Anna Marie, 1994. *New Right Discourse on Race and Sexuality: Britain, 1968–1990*, Cambridge: Cambridge University Press.

Spivak, Gayatri Chakravorty, 1994. *Outside in the Teaching Machine*, London, New York: Routledge.

Tabili, Laura, 1994. *'We Ask for British Justice': Workers and Racial Difference in Late Imperial Britain*, Ithaca: Cornell University Press.

Thatcher, Margaret, 1997. *The Collected Speeches*, London: HarperCollins.

Tölölyan, Khachig, 1991. 'The Nation-State and Its Others: In Lieu of a Preface,' *Diaspora* 1(1), 3–7.

Trouillot, Michel-Rolph, 1990. *Haiti, State against Nation: The Origins and Legacy of Duvalierism*, New York: Monthly Review Press.

Young, Iris Marion, 1990. 'The Ideal of Community and the Politics of Difference,' in Linda Nicholson, ed., *Feminism/Postmodernism*, London, New York: Routledge, 300–23.

Instrumental and Synoptic Dimensions of Interdisciplinarity in Postcolonial Studies

ATO QUAYSON

IF THE PAPERS GIVEN at the 1997 MLA meeting in Toronto attest to the vogue for interdisciplinarity in academic circles, then the tendency amongst critics to conjure strange titles for their essays also signals a desire to disrupt normal boundaries in the quest for a more inclusive perspective – consider 'The Architextual Structures of James Joyce's Ulysses: Colonised Homes, Hegemonic Schools, National Taverns, and Heterotopic Brothels' or 'Limit of the Nation: The Hymen and Griselda's Smock' from a programme on *Chaucer's Queer Nation*.[1] In its wide usage, the term 'interdisciplinary' itself proliferates a number of confusions which turn on the issue of what exactly such work in the sciences and the arts entails. In her book *Interdisciplinarity: History, Theory, and Practice* (1990), Julie Thompson Klein designates a range of possible strategies: engaging in collaborative problem-solving; bridge-building between disciplines that remain discrete; developing synthetic theories that operate across disciplines; constituting new fields from overlapping areas of separate disciplines; borrowing metaphors and procedures across disciplines. The first category refers to instrumental interdisciplinarity, designed to intervene in specific problems in the world outside academia, while the others which collate ideas either for the constitution of different disciplines or in the application of a synthetic theory across disciplines, may be defined as 'synoptic inter-disciplinarity'. The peculiarity of the last category is that it appears to be geared towards addressing concerns in its 'home' discipline, even when borrowing liberally from others.

This trend is most noticeable when a particular interdisciplinary model is thought to be new and untested. Such was the case with Gillian Beer's *Darwin's Plots:*[2] originally thought of as a work on literature, it came to be regarded as a major contribution to the history of science. So too the theories of Bakhtin or Foucault or Edward Said

---

[1] Information from a review of the 1997 MLA conference in the *Times Higher Educational Supplement* (January 9, 1998).

[2] See Gillian Beer, *Darwin's Plots: Evolutionary Narrative in Darwin, George Eliot and Nineteenth-Century Fiction* (London: Routledge & Kegan Paul, 1983).

are not reducible to any single discipline and have had an impact on many other fields. Some writers such as Jorge Luis Borges are notoriously interdisciplinary in their approach to their creative writing, and the same boundary transgressions characterize books as different as C.L.R. James's *Beyond a Boundary* (cricket history, biography, cultural studies, epic), Amitav Ghosh's *In an Antique Land* (ethnography, biography, travel narrative, Egyptology and epic) and Charles Van Onselen's monumental *The Seed is Mine: The Life of Kas Maine* (history, political science, anthropology, biography, epic).[3] There are, however, wide areas of overlap between the instrumental and the synoptic definitions for the obvious reason that both require a constant dialogue between the contiguous disciplines (see Klein: 41–4; 55–73). Furthermore, both types of interdisciplinarity are ultimately concerned with intervening in the constitution of reality, even when this proceeds from a primary engagement with texts and concepts rather than with the real world itself.

How are these considerations of instrumental and synoptic interdisciplinarity to be applied to postcolonial studies? And how are we to trace the implications of the interdisciplinary paradigm for a field whose social referent is a peculiarly anguished domain that is *post-colonial* both in the sense of coming problematically after colonialism, and *post*colonial in the sense of struggling to transcend the effects of colonialism through an engaged and situated practice?[4] Postcolonial studies, which in their turn have influenced other enquiries, are highly interdisciplinary in the synoptic sense, borrowing freely from a wide range of fields to challenge received assumptions. The Igbos have a saying that when the world is dancing, it is impossible to see it in perspective by standing still; and it is often argued that postcolonial critiques must move across boundaries in order to understand the complex relations secreted during the processes of colonialism and in its aftermath. At the end of his insightful essay 'Blurred Genres: The Refiguration of Social Thought', the anthropologist Clifford Geertz

[3] C.L.R. James, *Beyond a Boundary* (1963; London: Serpent's Tail, 1994); Amitav Ghosh, *In an Antique Land* (London: Granta, 1992); Charles Van Onselen, *The Seed is Mine: The Life of Kas Maine, A South African Sharecropper 1894–1985* (Oxford: James Currey).

[4] The debate about the 'post' in post-colonial has raged over the pages of numerous articles and journals. See for example Anne McClintock's 'The Angel of Progress: Pitfalls of the Term "Postcolonial"', *Social Text* 31/32 (1992), 84–98, Peter Childs and Patrick Williams, *An Introduction to Post-Colonial Theory* (London: Prentice Hall/Harvester Wheatsheaf, 1997).

maintains that the blurring of genres in interdisciplinary studies also produces a blurring of the roles that are normally seen to apply to scientists and cultural critics in their different pursuits.[5] Hence his suggestion that clarity is necessary to gauge the forms of action to be derived from interdisciplinarity, is one that is relevant to postcolonial studies, where the social referents press for instrumental solutions and not merely for imaginative recastings of old problems.

My aim in this essay is to explore whether academic interdisciplinarity offers or forecloses the possibility of social engagement with the postcolonial world outside the academy. To assess the potentialities and weaknesses in postcolonial interdisciplinarity, I will offer situated readings of two theoretical texts which defamiliarize both constituted disciplinary boundaries as well as the 'everyday': Achille Mbembe's 'Provisional Notes on the African Postcolony'[6] and Homi Bhabha's 'Signs Taken for Wonders: Questions of Ambivalence and Authority under a Tree outside Delhi, May 1817'.[7] Mbembe's concern is the everyday of the riddled political existence of people under the domination of tyrannical regimes in postcolonial Africa. For Bhabha the everyday object – the book – becomes in the context of colonialism a surrogate of much more. But I begin with a reading of two short passages from Theodor Adorno, a thinker who proceeds from epistemological foundations not emulated by Mbembe and Bhabha. For Adorno, everyday phenomena and concepts are negated in the interest of an estrangement that is ultimately instrumental rather than merely synoptic.[8] Passages from *Minima Moralia* manifest his procedure of consolidating aphorisms. Much of his work, and that of the Frankfurt School more generally, was written as a vigorous analysis of the peculiar development of totally administered societies with its culmination in German fascism. Frankfurtian critical theory commenced before the victory of Nazism and continually addressed the slide of the working class into chauvinism, racism and reaction, and the loss of momentum for a historical socialist project in Germany. Here Adorno's

---

[5] Clifford Geertz, *Local Knowledge: Further Essays in Interpretive Anthropology* (New York: Basic Books, 1983), 35.
[6] Achille Mbembe, 'Provisional Notes on the African Postcolony', *Africa* 62 (1992), 3–37. Mbembe's essay was re-reprinted under a new title, 'The Banality of Power and the Aesthetics of Vulgarity in the Postcolony', *Public Culture* 4.2 (1992), 1–30. A debate appeared in *Public Culture* 5.1 (1992) together with his response, 'Prosaics of Servitude and Authoritarian Civilities', pp. 123–45.
[7] Homi Bhabha *The Location of Culture* (London: Routledge, 1994,) 102–22.
[8] Theodor Adorno, *Minima Moralia: Reflections from a Damaged Life* (1951; London: Verso, 1978).

work can be seen as an instance of a conjunctural theory whose social referent is a disillusioned social, cultural and political sphere, albeit in a Western Europe very different from anything we might discern in the contemporary postcolonial world. His writing shows the value of rigorously dissociating critical thought from the paradigms of established cognitive systems. Various critics are now fruitfully exploring the uses of Adorno's thought for postcolonial studies.[9]

Adorno and the Negations of the Everyday

I am deliberately going to read the passages from *Minima Moralia* out of context,[10] while attempting to filter into view those other aspects of Adorno's life and work that may help us grasp the nature of his aphoristic thinking. In the preface to the book he grants that 'dialectical theory, abhorring anything isolated, cannot admit aphorisms as such', but then adds that 'if today the subject is vanishing, aphorisms take upon themselves the duty "to consider the evanescent itself as essential"' (16). In his practice, the 'essential' is not to be confused with the observed phenomenon which often forms the trigger for his reflections, but is that which makes itself manifest only after the phenomenon is explored in terms of its contradictory structure.[11]

[9] The most sustained attempt to think through the implications of Adorno for postcolonial studies has been that of Asha Varadharajan in *Exotic Parodies: Subjectivity in Adorno, Said and Spivak* (Minneapolis: University of Minnesota Press, 1995), 43; 55–66. See also Neil Lazarus, 'Modernism and Modernity: T.W. Adorno and Contemporary South African Literature', *Cultural Critique* 5 (1987), 131–56 and R. Radhakrishnan, 'The Changing Subject and Politics of Theory', *Differences* 2.2 (1990), 126–52 for illuminating discussions of Adorno in the context of postcolonial concerns.

[10] For accounts of the development of Adorno's thought and of the critical theory of the Frankfurt School more generally see Martin Jay, *The Dialectical Imagination: A History of the Frankfurt School and the Institute of Social Research, 1923–50* (Toronto and Boston: Little and Brown, 1973); Fredric Jameson, *Late Marxism: Adorno, or, The Persistence of the Dialectic* (London and New York: Verso, 1990); Andrew Arato and Eike Gebhardt, *The Essential Frankfurt School Reader* (New York: Continuum, 1997); and Simon Jarvis, *Adorno* (Cambridge: Polity Press), 1998.

[11] This feature of his writings rests on his idea of the non-identity between the subject and the object or of concepts and objects. The most sustained exposition of this idea is to be found in his *Negative Dialectics* (New York: Seabury Press, 1973). See also Martin Jay's exposition of Adorno's views on totality in 'Theodor Adorno and the Collapse of the Lukácsian Concept of

The passages entitled 'Refuge for the Homeless' (no. 18) and 'Do not Knock' (no. 19) in *Minima Moralia* demonstrate these concepts. The first begins with an examination of the problematic status of human dwelling where each trait of comfort is a musty pact of family interests paid for by a betrayal of knowledge: 'Dwelling, in the proper sense, is now impossible.' Adorno leaves this curious meditation unclarified. Instead he goes on to suggest that the functional modern habitation (centrally planned housing) is nothing but the intrusion of mechanical reproduction into the sphere of modern living. It is 'devoid of all relation to the occupant', much like 'factory sites that have strayed into the consumption sphere'. Adorno then turns his attention to the organization of sleeping space, observing that people require beds so close to the ground that the threshold between waking and dreaming seems to have been abolished. This has sinister implications, since the apparent abolition of the threshold between sleeping and waking is precisely to allow the worker to be on call at any hour, 'alert and unconscious at once'. These disjunctures do not impact solely on the working classes because even the attempt to 'evade responsibility for one's own residence by moving into a hotel or furnished rooms', is nothing but a rehearsal of 'enforced conditions of emigration'. (Here one senses that his own alienation from his native Germany because of anti-semitic persecutions is being globalized into an existential condition.)

Adorno then points out that, as always, the people that most suffer are those that have no or little choice:

> They live, if not in slums, in bungalows that by tomorrow may be leaf-huts, trailers, cars, camps, or the open air. The house is past. The bombings of European cities, as well as the labour and concentration camps, merely proceed as executors, with what the immanent development of technology had long decided was to be the fate of houses.

This defines a process implicit in the domestic nuclear family unit and explicit in the tragic individuation and aloneness of homelessness. It is the ultimate result of a technology that inverts personal and social evolution, and is itself transmogrified into weapons of mass destruction.

Through a series of startling disjunctures, Adorno's focus on an everyday concept such as the dwelling opens out to reveal the abiding

Totality', in *Marxism and Totality: The Adventures of a Concept from Lukács to Habermas* (Cambridge: Polity Press, 1984); and, for a more elaborate account of Adorno's dialectical approach, see Jameson 1990.

logic of late capitalism and its scientific corollary, technology. If we ignore for the moment his formulations for living under such conditions and move on to the next meditation in 'Do not Knock', we see the extension of Adorno's ideas about the distortions imposed by technology on the individual's relationship to objective reality, now focused on the automatization of human gestures within the domestic sphere. Once again he concentrates on mundane phenomena; here, the topic is how people relate to doors, which they seem unable to close quietly and discreetly. 'Technology is making gestures precise and brutal, and with them, men . . . It expels from movements all hesitation, deliberation, civility.' Technology supplies an apparent freedom in allowing people to disregard their usual surroundings; the cost is that by the law of pure functionality 'things assume a form that limits contact with them to a mere operation'. This is actually a form of unfreedom, because things now have no surplus, nothing which would survive in the core of experience. Hence the objective functionality of the everyday is entirely consumed in the immediate moment, thereby perpetuating the mechanical reflexes of capitalist production. The direct and tragic implication of this is that 'The new human type cannot be properly understood without awareness of what he is continuously exposed to from the world of things about him, even in his most secret innervations.' Here Adorno expresses in his peculiar way the inextricable existential relation between human subjectivity and its surrounding objects. For Adorno, the automatization of everyday life is no mere irritation but represents the complete dominance of a technological totality.

Adorno is concerned with the effects of technology when it is aligned to the petrified state systems of capitalism or fascism. It is here that as Joseph Rothschild argues in *Ethnopolitics*, ethnicity takes a political intensity in the modern world precisely because it is sometimes thought to be a bulwark against this threat, fulfilling that

> need for some psychological distance and social autonomy from the technocratic rationality that fuels the scientific modernization process, catalyzes its contradictions and conflicts, and thereby prompts the politicization of ethnicity.[12]

Even though the problems Adorno focuses on in *Minima Moralia* seem to pertain mainly to individual subjectivity, his interest proceeds from an

---

[12] Joseph Rothschild, *Ethnopolitics: A Conceptual Framework* (New York: Columbia University Press, 1981), 5.

intense concern with class relations. Hence when he analyses the constitutive negations within everyday phenomena he aims at liberating the phenomena from their existing ideological and class conditions. A dialectical structure is brought into view as part and parcel of a larger process of history. When Adorno triggers an aphorism, therefore, this is not in the service of existential cliche but its opposite. He concentrates on the quotidian so that, by a process of rapid and frenetic discursive negations, it is defamiliarized in the service of a larger critique of society. Thus a rigorous dialectical reasoning is allied to an exploration of the everyday which is simultaneously recognized, disturbed and apprehended as not at one with itself.

Even though his procedures might seem amenable to absorption into a postmodernist anti-systemic rationality, we should note that Adorno is not opposed to totality and universals as concepts. As Jameson observes, Adorno presupposes a totality (normally construed as late capitalism or the totally administered society). His focus on the phenomenon 'unexpectedly addresses that totality itself and modifies it, not the particular that was its pretext'. Its inalienable flipside is that the thematization of totality 'that drew in this or that isolated historical particular as a mere example or illustration proves itself to have been a subterfuge for the striking modification, the interpretation by way of shock and novelty, of the putative example itself' (Jameson 1990: 33).

Adorno's aphoristic method, and his dialectical analysis of the everyday phenomenon, are then ultimately elements of a critique of capitalist society. 'The only philosophy which can be responsibly practised in face of despair is the attempt to contemplate all things as they would present themselves from the standpoint of redemption' (Finale). It is useful to understand redemption here as social emancipation and to note that in this formulation we get an echo of Marx's view that there is no individual emancipation without that of society. In *Negative Dialectics* this essential methodological premise is glossed more fully:

> The dialectical mediation of the universal and the particular does not allow a theory that opts for the particular to treat the universal overzealously as a soap bubble. If it did that, theory, would be incapable of registering the pernicious supremacy of the universal in the current state of things in which the universal would find itself stripped of its bad particularity insofar as individuals were restored to what rightly belonged to them. Nor are on the other hand conceptions of a transcendental subject acceptable, a subject without society and without those individuals whom for good or ill it integrates. (*Negative Dialectics*, 199–200)

How do we conceptualize instrumental and synoptic interdisciplinarity in the light of Adorno's distinctive conceptual presuppositions? Adorno considers everyday reality to be too multifarious and complex to be addressed from a single perspective, but his methodology is not interdisciplinary in the straightforward sense of integrating different disciplines. The interdisciplinarity lies rather in the manner in which concepts are shifted rapidly between universalized and particularized perspectives in such a way that these are not amenable to easy appropriation by any single disciplinary perspective without recourse to the simultaneous undoing of such a perspective. Crucially, the exploration of concepts is grounded in everyday reality. Thus it is that Adorno's interdisciplinary methodology is on the one hand synoptic in forcing a multifocal perspective, and on the other hand instrumental in that it forces a perception of abstract concepts in their concrete and particular phenomenal and cultural articulations. By means of the 'suddenness' of his methodological shifts he simultaneously allows an aligment of perception to critique, so that the perception is not merely of a datum of lived experience, but is also evaluative in terms of a more critical engagement with the forms of capitalist social organization.

Achille Mbembe and the Banalities of Power

In Achille Mbembe's essay, 'Provisional Notes on the African Post-colony' some of the themes discussed above reemerge. This is not to suggest that Mbembe is influenced by Adorno, but rather to observe the different parameters of Mbembe's disruption of the everyday. Here the focus is not on individual phenomena and abstract concepts but on assumptions about the lived experience of ordinary Africans as their subjectivity is enacted in the public sphere. Moreover Adorno's notion of what Neil Lazarus describes as 'the implacable hegemony of the total administration',[13] is replaced by an interest in how such systems are confirmed and deconstructed, since in the lives of the populace, a simultaneous assertion and disruption of state authority is manifest. And although Mbembe is concerned to expose the antinomic structure of the everyday, this is not in the service of a higher critique of political economy, but as a means of dissolving the dichotomies between state and civil society in the constitution of subjectivity. Traces of Foucault

[13] Lazarus 1987: 135.

and Bakhtin, Gramsci, Bataille and even Habermas are discernible in an essay where the central concern is with 'the banality of power'. In Mbembe's terms, banality does not merely signify the ways in which bureaucratic formalities are routinized, but refers directly to those elements of the obscene and the grotesque. These in Bakhtin's formulations are located in 'non-official' cultures while being intrinsic to all systems of domination' (3).

If his identification of the obscene and the grotesque as immanent in specific systems of domination may appear exorbitant, he adduces evidence of the various ways in which postcolonial African leaders regularly focus on the hedonistic satiation of the body as a means of foregrounding their power. This is governed by a specific dynamic of public rituals, seen most effectively in

the rounds of administrative authorities, their discursive perform-ances, ceremonies and banquets, official visits of foreign dignitaries, national holidays, presentations of medals, radio and press commun-ications, tax collection; ordinary interactions between citizens, the police and bureaucracy, school teachers and pupils, husbands and wives, church leaders and their flock.

We should note that in discussing African politics in a scatological register, Mbembe indavertently suppresses the history of how this was developed in the West and continues to be deployed as a stereotype in documentaries, news bulletins and general opinions about Africa beamed across the world. This is critical because even as Western governments were lampooning the likes of Mobutu, Bokassa, and Amin, they were propping up their corrupt regimes both financially and militarily in the service of Cold War strategic planning. But whereas the scatological register has a geneaology whose implications ramify well beyond the area delimited by Mbembe, the body also provides metaphors by which the popular imagination attempts to subvert the discourses of power. Here the Gramscian notion of hegemony is located in a peculiarly different way: whereas consent and coercion go hand in hand in the totalitarian African postcolony, identification with the politically dominant authorities is evaded. Mbembe elaborates the extent to which ordinary people, through linguistic devices involving puns, innuendoes and direct misinterpreta-tions of official discourses, discompose political slogans and ideas into tropes of sexual and bodily functions.

But it is in elaborating his notion of the unstable relation between coercion and consent that the specificities of Membe's interdisciplinary model becomes evident. In attempting to describe the distinctive features of the African postcolony, he notes that it is 'a specific system of signs, a particular way of fabricating simulacra or re-forming stereotypes' (3). Mbembe is evidently influenced by poststructuralist theories which link images, stereotypes and power. This seems to place him squarely among those who conflate the power-laden effects of real life events with the devices and import of textuality, hence rendering the real world graspable in essentially textual terms. But Mbembe adds another dimension that undermines this textualized and sign-oriented definition of postcolonial Africa. For this entity is not 'just an economy of signs in which power is mirrored and *imagined* self-reflectively' since it is further characterised by

> a distinctive style of political improvisation, by a tendency towards excess and a lack of proportion as well as by a distinctive style in which identities are multiplied, transformed and put into circulation . . . What distinguishes the postcolony from other regimes of violence and domination is not only the luxuriousness of style and the down-to-earth realism that characterise its power, or even the fact that it is particularly raw power that it prefers to exercise; peculiar also to the postcolony is the way the relationship between rulers and ruled is forged by means of a specific practice: simulacrum (*le simulacre*). (10)

And yet, as he states earlier,

> the signs, vocabulary and narratives that it produces are not meant merely to be symbols; they are officially invested with a surplus of meanings which are not negotiable and which one is officially forbidden to depart from or challenge. So as to ensure that no such challenge takes place, the champions of state power invent entire constellations of ideas; they adopt a distinct set of cultural repertoires and powerfully evocative concepts; but they also have resort, if necessary, to the systematic application of pain. (4)

We see in such a formulation the uneasy recognition that the seeming symbolic nexus of gaining consent always has a potential for being short-circuited by the intrusion of force. This configuration of items ensures that the means of subversion, of the banalization of the discourses of authority in the hands of the ordinary people, has to take an especially subtle edge. And that is why the discourses of power are subverted from within their own symbolic regime and repertoires and not from without.

What is to be extrapolated from Mbembe's specific interdisciplinary configuration? He carefully avoids centring his discussion on either the separate domains of excessive actions of political authorities, or on the subtle activities of subversion generated by ordinary people. As he points out early in the essay, he is keen to avoid simple binary categories used in standard interpretations of domination such as resistance v. passivity, autonomy v. subjection. However, to side-step these binarisms, he is also obliged to suggest a certain equivalence in the production and circulation of signs between the political authorities and the ordinary people. This is suggested in his argument that though it is those in power who frequently engender the symbols and rituals of authorization, these are quickly wrested and rendered 'commonplace' through the active participation of the populace in their proliferation and subsequent transformation. But his production of equivalence can be seen as operating at another level because he also parallels the domain of the aesthetic with the political, reading both through the interdisciplinary theoretical model he has devised by crossing Gramsci, Foucault and Bakhtin. It is not insignificant that the version of his paper published in the United States is entitled 'The Banality of Power and the Aesthetics of Vulgarity in the Postcolony', nor that he frequently refers to Sony Labou Tansi's novel *La Vie et demie* for examples about the corruption of the political elites which he puts at par with the reports taken from national newspapers in Cameroon.[14] In other words, fiction and fact are put on the same footing when discussing the realities of consent and coercion, both, as he notes elsewhere, contributing to the 'configuration of reality'. This then allows a simultaneous reading of the literary/aesthetic as political and the political as literary/aesthetic.

One of Mbembe's key analytic strategies is to deploy a cultural studies approach for the elaboration of political subjectivity in the African postcolony. In this process he avoids the normal development-orientated discourses of the political sciences and encourages an

---

[14] On the limitations of such equivalence between literary texts and other domains, see Tejumola Olaniyan, 'Narrativizing Postcoloniality: Responsibilities', *Public Culture* 5.1 (1992), 47–55. Olaniyan opens his essay by first showing how texts like Soyinka's *Opera Wonyosi* seem to prefigure Mbembe's scatological discussion of the postcolony. But he goes on to show the radical differences between the two writers and the weaknesses in Mbembe's dissolution of binarisms and his pursuit of equivalences between different domains in their place.

engagement with ideas and realities that can only be joined via a comparative methodology. Nevertheless, it is precisely in his innovative reformulation of political theory in the light of cultural studies that his interdisciplinary model founders. For even though his procedure is clearly synoptic, his method of analysis still forecloses the imaginative possibility of transcending the dilemmas of civil society he is addressing. This must not be mistaken as a call for critics to proffer solutions to intractable problems; yet it remains the case that Mbembe sidesteps issues of antagonism and places the discussion of the relation between the dominated and their oppressors in an idiom that ends up obscuring both the sources of effective political power, and how it might be appropriated in the interests of the people. Although he notes the constant presence of a potential for state violence and instances its actualization, neither the idea of violence nor the people's responses is integrated into the discussion. Thus subversion is constantly caught within the regulative parameters allowed by the state, as if this cannot be expressed in any form of political struggle or antagonism. As Tejumola Olaniyan rightly points out, the organized challenges of the dominated are rendered peripheral by Mbembe:

> the emphasis should be not only on the stated logics as Mbembe recommends, but also on the equally important logics of how that epistemological field is the site and stake of most often agonistic and unequal struggles among different groups over its definition, structure, and character; how it is perpetually, with varying degrees of failure or success by unsteady alliances, restructured, realigned, revisioned, consolidated, etc.[15]

By rendering a series of equivalences both in terms of the subject matter and in the method of its description, Mbembe precludes discussion of the postcolony as a terrain of life and death struggles which in political science studies and standard commentaries on Africa are figured in famines, disease, civil wars and refugees. Instead he focuses on persistent and seemingly peaceful modes of subversion. But if the insights of his interdisciplinary model are to be further elaborated, they would have to be joined to an analysis of such struggles against material deprivation and totalitarian oppression. The question is whether the special dynamics of which Mbembe speaks might lead to positive change in the physical and social world; and this concern

[15] Olaniyan 1992: 51.

should not be seen as a supplement to his fertile kind of synoptic interdisciplinarity, but as an integral part of it.

Homi Bhabha: Interdisciplinarity as Catachresis

If Adorno and Mbembe allow us to view the everyday either as not at one with itself or as part of a fractious simultaneity of domination and subversion, in Bhabha's work the defamiliarizing work is applied to the objects of discussion, while the conceptual categories brought to bear on these in the first place, are subjected to a constant process of deconstructive dissolution and re-aggregation. In Adorno's hands aphorism is the conduit for disrupting clichéd modes of thought in order that the antinomic structure of the everyday phenomenon or idea illuminates a larger movement of negativity in history. For Mbembe, the everyday of political existence is the site for a series of mutualities between the *commandement* and its reception by the ordinary people in such a way that the everyday becomes the simultaneous assertion and disaffirmation of the discourses of power. With Bhabha something different takes place. In his writing, an apparent aphoristic structure generates what I would describe as 'quotationality', a clumsy neologism I use to distinguish his procedure from that of Adorno where the aphorisms can be quoted out of context (and frequently are), but are so well grounded within a coherent movement of thought, that when returned to their original environment, their status as an aspect of this context is apparent. In Bhabha's case 'quotationality' serializes aphorisms without allowing them to be properly situated, a manoeuvre characteristic of a model which refuses the possibility of any totality, and oscillates so rapidly between different disciplinary boundaries that their borders are blurred. Thus whereas his writings on the colonial encounter imply sentiments of considerable ethical intensity, no precise location for that intensity is consolidated.

Bhabha opens 'Signs Taken for Wonders' with a setting that prepares for a tropological reading of power:

> There is a scene in the cultural writings of English colonialism which repeats so insistently after the early nineteenth century – and, through that repetition, so triumphantly inaugurates a literature of empire – that I am bound to repeat it once more. It is a scenario played out in the wild and wordless wastes of colonial Africa, the Caribbean, of sudden, fortuitous discovery of the English book. It is

like all myths of origin, memorable for its balance between epiphany and enunciation. The discovery of the book is, at once, a moment of originality and authority. It is, as well, a process of displacement that, paradoxically, makes the presence of the book wondrous to the extent to which it is repeated, translated, misread, displaced. It is with the emblem of the English book – 'signs taken for wonders' – as an insignia of colonial authority and a signifier of colonial desire and discipline, that I want to begin this chapter. (102)

The notion of a 'primal scene' is reiterated first in relation to an Indian catechist Anund Messeh and his attempts to convince a group of Indians that when read in a Brahminical light, the Bible was the Word of God; second in Marlow's discovery of Towson's (or Towser's) *Inquiry Into Some Points of Seamanship* in Conrad's *Heart of Darkness*; and third in V.S. Naipaul's reflections on the same passage from Conrad. These three encounters are read as enunciatory of significations beyond their immediate contexts, the implication being that 'The discovery of the book institutes the sign of appropriate representation: the word of God, truth, art, creates the conditions for beginning a practice of history and narrative' (105). Bhabha's abstractions seem concerned with questions of narrative; the three instances of the book's discovery are epiphanic moments that trigger particular inventions of selfhood.

But Bhabha does not rest at that, and he goes on to make a startling assertion: 'For despite the accident of discovery, the repetition of the emergence of the book, represents important moments in the historical transformation and the discursive configuration of the colonial text and context' (105). For, he claims, the discovery of the book exposes the discourse of civil address, and, in so doing, reveals a particular entailment of books and their manifestation with the wider processes of colonialism. Thus, with respect to Anund Messeh, his 'lifeless repetition of chapter and verse, his artless technique of translation, participate in one of the most artful technologies of colonial power' (16). In the case of Marlow, the book he discovers 'is the book of work that turns delirium into the discourse of civil address' (op. cit.); while with Naipaul, his attempt to translate Conrad from Africa to the Caribbean registers an urge 'to transform the despair of postcolonial history into an appeal for the autonomy of art' (107).

Bhabha then proceeds to shift 'the book' from its ordinary material parameters into the domain of colonialist discourse, and in doing this, he interprets the book as having determinative political effects in establishing and maintaining colonialism. The book becomes an

embodiment, almost a colonial body in itself. At times it is described as
if its mere existence endows it with a specific form of agency tied to the
colonial enterprise. This is never stated explicitly but is allowed to
gather implication incrementally. Thus he writes:

> If these scenes, as I have narrated them, suggest the triumph of the
> writ of colonialist power, then it must be conceded that the wily
> letter of the law inscribes a much more ambivalent text of authority.
> For it is in-between the edict of Englishness and the assault of the
> dark unruly spaces of the earth, through an act of repetition, that the
> colonial text emerges uncertainly.

At this stage we might pause to ask how 'the discovery of the book' is
turned into the 'triumph of the writ', 'the wily letter of the law' and 'the
ambivalent text of authority'? The rest of Bhabha's essay is devoted to
deconstructing the nature of colonial authority and showing how its
authoritative discourse always harbours essential contradictions that
undermine it both from within itself and from the context of the
colonial encounter.

   If the process of unpacking this essay proves frustrating, it is the
precise effect that this mode of interdisciplinarity invites: Bhabha
focuses on a putatively concrete object, the book, but de-materializes
it by discussing it as an abstraction. At the same time, and quite
contradictorily, he is interested in retaining the materiality of the book
in order to deconstruct the logocentrism of colonialist authority:
'Consequently, the colonial presence is always ambivalent, split
between its appearance as original and authoritative and its articulation as repetition and difference' (107). And yet at no time does he
discuss instances of colonial authority in terms of colonial persons and
authority figures who are present only by the proxy of the book.

   Bhabha's writings have been criticized by many commentators,
perhaps none more perceptive than Bart Moore-Gilbert.[16] For

[16] Bhabha's writing has drawn a lot of sharp criticism by people pursuing
different methodologies. See, for example, Arif Dirlik, 'The Postcolonial Aura:
Third World Criticism in the Age of Global Capitalism', *Critical Inquiry* 20.2
(1994), 328–56; Neil Lazarus, 'Disavowing Decolonization: Fanon, Nationalism, and the Problematic of Representation in Current Theories of Colonial
Discourse', *Research in African Literatures* 24.4 (1993), 69–98; Abdul JanMohamed, 'The Economy of Manichean Allegory: The Function of Racial
Difference in Colonialist Literature', *Critical Inquiry* 12.1 (1985), 59–87;
Masao Miyoshi, 'A Borderless World? From Colonialism to Transnationalism
and the Decline of the Nation-State', *Critical Inquiry* 19 (1993), 726–51; Laura

Moore-Gilbert, the problems with Bhabha's analysis do not lie merely in the way he conflates psychology with politics, nor his reading of the symbolic as the political. Rather Moore-Gilbert argues that Bhabha fails to question the apparent Eurocentric bias of some of the Freudian and Lacanian psychoanalytic paradigms he uses; and his reading of Fanon omits the careful historicization of the psychological phenomena to be examined: 'What sometimes seems to get lost in Bhabha's homogenizing and transhistorical model of the mutual (mis)recognitions of all cultures is Fanon's insistence that the psychic economy of colonialism mediates material, historically grounded, relations of power.'[17] For Moore-Gilbert the questions Bhabha raises – such as 'the varied patterns and expressions of affective structures like ambivalence' which can only be explained in diachronic terms – 'can indeed be answered, but only by a differential engagement with the complex histories and material processes of which imperialism is made up' (151).

What is the value of Bhabha's form of interdisciplinarity? Crossing Derrida, Lacan and Foucault, he seeks to address several audiences simultaneously, but in such a way as not to be recognizably tied to any single discipline. Thus in the fertile way in which he reads tropes, his work seems to be aimed at literary theory; in the febrile 'nervous conditions' of the encounter between the colonizer and the colonized which he attempts to formulate, his work appears to address psychoanalysis; in his postulation of these encounters as being between subjects situated in a putative history whose lineaments are recognizably those of the colonial era in India and elsewhere, he gestures towards historians. Yet his is a narrative which resolutely resists assimilation into a holistic picture. Bhabha produces a catachrestic discourse in which the various ideas he puts together deliberately generate a 'misfit', a deliberately non-integrated and continually mobile series of positions and ideas that are meant to mime the very labile processes he is at pains to describe. His language, though seemingly aphoristic, has the restless quality of proliferating a series of discrete observations which refuse to cohere into a perspectival whole, sowing permanent doubt in the reader as to whether it has all been fully understood.

This brings us to an issue of critical significance: what does

Chrisman, 'The Imperial Unconscious? Representations of Imperial Discourse', *Critical Quarterly* 32.3 (1990), 38–58; and Benita Parry, 'Signs of Our Times', *Third Text* 28/29 (1994), 5–24.

[17] Moore-Gilbert, *Post-Colonial Theory: Contexts, Practices, Politics* (London: Verso, 1997), 147.

interdisciplinarity provide both for our understanding of postcolonial relations and, more importantly, for the ways in which we might address postcolonial questions as a project engaging theories, and paradigms?[18] It could seem pretentious in this phase of postmodern angst to raise this question at all. What right, a cynic might ask, do postcolonial intellectuals working in Western universities have to intervene in the real life crises of the postcolony? And on whose behalf would they be doing this, their paymasters or of the postcolonials themselves? And if these questions are not resolvable, why be concerned with the implications of the knowledge produced by postcolonial interdisciplinarity? The project of postcolonialism, if indeed there is thought to be one, is always entangled with ethical questions since it seems to me impossible to discuss the negative effects of colonialism past and present without implicitly or explicitly making known the ethical value of the revisions and rewritings – a much more anguished and pressing question than say in the study of Milton, since the postcolony is a palpable affect wherever we find ourselves. What, for instance, is one to make of the hanging of Ken Saro-Wiwa when teaching his novel *Sozaboy* or viewing his TV series *Basi and Co.*? To my mind, the realities of the world and the domain of discourse seem impossible to separate and any move to do so can only create reified forms of knowledge.

Thus, the interdisciplinary model has ultimately to answer to the ways in which it shapes an ethical attitude to reality, in this case, to postcolonial reality. Here Adorno's defamiliarizations of the everyday become pertinent. His methodology alerts us to the pitfalls of complacency in our engagement with seemingly innocent everyday concepts; and his practice of defamiliarization is directed at raising our consciousness of the extent to which everyday phenomena are over-determined by world-historical processes that are occluded in traditional forms of philosophizing, and which under the violence of

---

[18] It has to be noted that several disciplines that have had to deal with postcolonial societies have had to stage some such debates between theory and practice. One of the most lively has been that taking place among African philosophers. See, for instance Paulin Hountondji, *African Philosophy: Myth and Reality*, trans. Henri Evans and Jonathan Rée (Bloomington: Indiana University Press, 1983) for an account of African philosophy as part of a larger system of theoretical reflections and Tsenay Serequeberhan, *The Hermeneutics of African Philosophy: Horizon and Discourse* (New York: Routledge, 1994) for an discussion of the need to constitute African philosophy as a form of praxis rather than just theory.

capitalism and the totally administered state lead to an atrophying of the spirit. With Mbembe, a radical perspective is not aligned directly to an ethical domain, despite the fact that he itemizes instances of violence and brutality. Furthermore because he situates the dominated and the dominating within the same epistemological sphere, and shows them to be entrapped in certain mutualities of subjectivity, the shock and anger that might have attended his model are short-circuited. The scale of power registered is dissipated by the model of analysis deployed; his paradigm of equivalence sheds light, but dissipates anger. In other words, there is a dramaturgical intensity in Mbembe's narrative that keeps the relation between the commandement and the people simultaneously in view, but also positions us as spectators ready to applaud the innovative intelligence of the people rather than be agitated by the subliminal violence to which they must continually respond. With Bhabha, something decidedly different takes place. There is a concerted refusal of totalization and through his energetic and almost delirious deconstructive strategies, every category gets discomposed. In his sometimes productive, sometimes obfuscating interdisciplinary procedures, the writing becomes self-referential and calls for judgement on its own terms. And because we are encouraged to contemplate the fact of colonial epistemic violence which is never stablized, we are placed within a theoretical loop: there is sound and fury, but can we grasp what this signifies or whether it signifies anything at all?

It is neither possible nor desirable to legislate which models of interdisciplinary configurations should be deployed in postcolonial studies. But one thing remains clear, that for the synoptic perspective to be of some instrumental value in a context of continuing anguish and confusion, we have to be rigorous and self-conscious about our interdiscplinary practices. Nicholas Thomas provides an apposite conclusion to this discussion:

> If there is something basically enabling and positive in the undoing of disciplinary boundaries, authoritative privileges and canonical sources and modes of presentation, it may nevertheless be too easy to celebrate this new fluidity, this new scope for exhilarating trespass . . . It remains important to argue about the effectiveness of different disciplinary technologies; about the politics of analytical strategies; about the appropriateness of particular theoretical languages.[19]

[19] Nicholas Thomas, *Colonialism's Culture: Anthropology, Travel and Government* (Cambridge: Polity Press, 1994), 19.

Works Cited

Adorno, Theodor, 1951. *Minima Moralia: Reflections from a Damaged Life*; London: Verso, 1978.

——, 1973. *Negative Dialectics*, New York: Seabury Press.

Arato, Andrew, and Eike Gebhardt, 1997. *The Essential Frankfurt School Reader*, New York: Continuum.

Beer, Gillian, 1983. *Darwin's Plots: Evolutionary Narrative in Darwin, George Eliot and Nineteenth-Century Fiction*, London: Routledge & Kegan Paul.

Bhabha, Homi K, 1994. *The Location of Culture*, London: Routledge.

Childs, Peter, and Patrick Williams, 1997. *An Introduction to Post-Colonial Theory*, London: Prentice Hall/Harvester Wheatsheaf.

Chrisman, Laura, 1990. 'The Imperial Unconscious? Representations of Imperial Discourse', *Critical Quarterly* 32.3, 38–58.

Dirlik, Arif, 1994. 'The Postcolonial Aura: Third World Criticism in the Age of Global Capitalism', *Critical Inquiry* 20.2, 328–56.

Geertz, Clifford, 1983. *Local Knowledge: Further Essays in Interpretive Anthropology*, New York: Basic Books.

Ghosh, Amitav, 1992. *In an Antique Land*, London: Granta.

Hountondji, Paulin, 1983. *African Philosophy: Myth and Reality*, trans. Henri Evans and Jonathan Rée, Bloomington: Indiana University Press.

James, C.L.R., 1963. *Beyond a Boundary*; London: Serpent's Tail, 1994.

——, 1993. 'Popular Arts and Modern Society', in *American Civilization*, ed. Anna Grimshaw and Keith Hart, Oxford: Blackwell, 135.

Jameson, Frederic,1990. *Late Marxism: Adorno, or, The Persistence of the Dialectic*, London and New York: Verso.

JanMohamed, Abdul, 1985. 'The Economy of Manichean Allegory: The Function of Racial Difference in Colonialist Literature', *Critical Inquiry* 12.1, 59–87.

Jarvis, Simon, 1998. *Adorno*, Cambridge: Polity Press.

Jay, Martin, 1973. *The Dialectical Imagination: A History of the Frankfurt School and the Institute of Social Research, 1923–50*, Toronto and Boston: Little and Brown.

——, 1984. 'Theodor Adorno and the Collapse of the Lukácsian Concept of Totality', in *Marxism and Totality: The Adventures of a Concept from Lukács to Habermas*, Cambridge: Polity Press.

Klein, Julie Thompson, 1990. *Interdisciplinarity: History, Theory, Practice*, Detroit: Wayne State University Press.

Lazarus, Neil, 1987. 'Modernism and Modernity: T.W. Adorno and Contemporary South African Literature', *Cultural Critique* 5, 131–56.

——, 1993. 'Disavowing Decolonization: Fanon, Nationalism, and the Problematic of Representation in Current Theories of Colonial Discourse', *Research in African Literatures* 24.4, 69–98.

Mbembe, Achille, 1992. 'Provisional Notes on the African Postcolony', *Africa* 62, 3–37.

——, 1992. 'Prosaics of Servitude and Authoritarian Civilities', *Public Culture* 5.1, 123–45.

——, 1992. 'The Banality of Power and the Aesthetics of Vulgarity in the Postcolony', *Public Culture* 4.2, 1–30.

McClintock, Anne, 1992. 'The Angel of Progress: Pitfalls of the Term "Postcolonial"', *Social Text* 31/32, 84–98.

——, 1997. *Imperial Leather: Race, Gender and Sexuality in the Colonial Contest*, London: Routledge.

Miyoshi, Masao, 1993. 'A Borderless World? From Colonialism to Transnationalism and the Decline of the Nation-State', *Critical Inquiry* 19, 726–51.

Moore-Gilbert, Bart, 1997. *Post-Colonial Theory: Contexts, Practices, Politics*, London: Verso.

Olaniyan, Tejumola, 1992. 'Narrativizing Postcoloniality: Responsibilities', *Public Culture* 5.1, 47–55.

Parry, Benita, 1994. 'Signs of Our Times', *Third Text* 28/29, 5–24.

Radhakrishnan, R, 1990. 'The Changing Subject and Politics of Theory', *Differences* 2.2, 126–52.

Rothschild, Joseph, 1981. *Ethnopolitics: A Conceptual Framework*, New York: Columbia University Press.

Serequeberhan, Tsenay, 1994. *The Hermeneutics of African Philosophy: Horizon and Discourse*, New York: Routledge.

Thomas, Nicholas, 1994. *Colonialism's Culture: Anthropology, Travel and Government*, Cambridge: Polity Press.

Times Higher Educational Supplement, January 9, 1998.

Van Onselen, Charles. *The Seed is Mine: The Life of Kas Maine, A South African Sharecropper 1894–1985*, Oxford: James Currey.

Varadharajan, Asha, 1995. *Exotic Parodies: Subjectivity in Adorno, Said and Spivak*, Minneapolis: University of Minnesota Press.

Indian and Irish Unrest in Kipling's Kim

TIM WATSON

CRITICAL ENGAGEMENTS with a fiction that has been described as 'the cult novel of high colonialism' (Nair 1995: 159), confirm the status of *Kim* as one of the central texts in the field of postcolonial studies.[1] Moreover, fictional rewritings of *Kim* bear witness to the novel's generative power and the symbolic importance of its hybrid hero: consider the protagonist's literary descendants in Rabindranath Tagore's *Gora*, Salman Rushdie's *Midnight's Children*, and Michael Ondaatje's *The English Patient*. My purpose, however, is to address the novel via a more detailed analysis of British and South Asian history than is usually attempted by literary scholars of Kipling. I will argue that in *Kim* we can see the work that the British put into constructing and defending the precarious terms, 'India' and 'the British Empire', which for many critics are the unexamined preconditions of their arguments. Close attention to the practices of British rule in India at the turn of the century will enable us to understand the ways in which declarations of the power and scope of the Raj, and, by extension, the whole imperial project, concealed and contained the assumption that threats to the British Empire would lead to its inevitable demise.

The peculiar logic of the Empire – a term that only came into general usage after the Indian Rebellion of 1857 and the Morant Bay uprising in Jamaica in 1865 – was that its period of greatest expansion was predicated on its eventual collapse. The premise of each new acquisition in Africa, every move to centralize and 'modernize' the apparatus of British rule in South Asia, was the need to defend British interests against challenges, both real and imagined, to that entity, the 'British Empire'. Paradoxically, the fictive unity of the Empire was in inverse proportion to the diversity of peoples and systems of administration contained within its unstable borders. In other words – to risk an overly

---

[1] Criticism of Kipling's novel that centres on the place of colonialism begins with Edmund Wilson's classic formulation of the conflict (or, rather, the lack of conflict) at the heart of *Kim* ('The Kipling That Nobody Read', 1941: 123–4). Other landmark essays on *Kim* are Parry (1972) and Said (1987); a representative sampling of other criticism would include Booker (1997), Chaudhuri (1957), Nair (1995), Randall (1996), Richards (1993), Wegner (1993–94), and Williams (1994).

neat formula for an inherently inconsistent and diverse set of historical processes – the end of the empire preceded, and even helped to produce, 'the Empire' as such. At the turn of the century, India was a particularly important site for this peculiar logic. As the largest, richest, and one of the longest established British territorial possessions, its strength or weakness symbolized the status of the British Empire as a whole. On the other hand, India was excluded from the dominant British narrative of colonies progressing towards 'mature' self-government. The anomalous position of India fractured the myth of a coherent empire, registered the power politics and economic rapacity behind the rapid imperial expansion of the last quarter of the nineteenth century, and revealed the justifications for the exploitation of 'backward peoples'.

In 1882, James Fitzjames Stephen, the liberal political theorist and legal scholar, issued a furious response to the proposed Ilbert Bill which would have allowed Indian judges to preside over some cases involving British defendants:

> It [the British Raj] is essentially an absolute government, founded, not on consent, but on conquest. It does not represent the native principles of life or of government, and it can never do so until it represents heathenism and barbarism . . . If . . . the authority of the Government is once materially relaxed . . . nothing but failure, anarchy, and ruin can be the result. (qtd. in Stokes 1959: 288, 303)

It would appear that the contemplation of the vast wealth and power of the British in India went hand in hand with forecasts and warnings of its ending, should authoritarian rule be compromised. The writer of an unsigned *Blackwood's Magazine* survey of the Raj since the Sepoy Revolt of 1857 boastfully proclaimed that 'the unbiassed impartiality of our rule' had removed 'all traces of 1857', but went on to argue, 'we shall remain for so long as we are able and strong enough to maintain our Empire; but if in process of time that Empire shall fall, nowhere will it disappear more swiftly or more completely than in our Eastern dependency, and leave not a wrack behind' ('India 1857' 1907: 619). This concern with the status of India can also be seen in more general writings on empire. In John Seeley's classic account of the development of British imperialism, *The Expansion of England* (1883), the loss of the Indian Empire is contemplated with a startling prescience:

> The moment a mutiny is but threatened, which shall be no mere mutiny, but the expression of a universal feeling of nationality, at that moment all hope is at an end . . . of preserving our Empire . . .

The moment India began really to show herself what we do idly imagine her to be, a conquered nation, that moment we should recognise perforce the impossibility of retaining her. And thus the mystic halo of marvel and miracle which has gathered round this Empire disppears before fixed scrutiny. (Seeley 1972: 185, 180)

Two years later, in 1885, the Indian National Congress was founded.

In this essay I will examine *Kim* as a work that engages with this logic of imperial expansion and collapse by containing and negating (but thereby representing) the dangers to British rule in both India and Ireland at the turn of the century. Kipling's novel, in which this unrest is an integral part of the imperial project itself, attempts to corral the figures of imperial peril and collapse – secret networks, paramilitary organizations, hostile foreign powers, the new language of anticolonial nationalism – and turn them into signs of the Empire's strength and flexibility.

The founding of the Indian National Congress signalled an emerging idea of an Indian nation, whose independent existence appeared to be hastened by the very practices of imperial rule designed to perpetuate Britain's domination: centralization of state apparatuses; more efficient communications; the wider dissemination of education, newspapers, and books; the rapid expansion of the railway system. British commentators and administrators were aware of the dangerous logic of their own political and cultural practices, and were at pains throughout the late nineteenth and early twentieth centuries to refute the power of Indian nationalism by denying that it possessed an adequate referent: in other words, 'India' did not exist. For example, in 1888 John Strachey in his book *India: Its Administration and Progress*, which became the standard work on the subject, proclaimed that: 'there is not, *and never was* an India, or even any country of India, possessing, according to European ideas, any sort of unity, physical, political, social, or religious; no Indian nation, no "people of India", of which we hear so much' (Strachey 1911: 5; emphasis in original). Following Ranajit Guha (1988), this is what we might call the prose of counter-insurgency: the careful negation of the categories in which the Indian unrest had begun to speak.

Strachey's text then refutes the manifesto of a nationalist movement which he never acknowledges, despite alluding to its reputed existence.[2] (I will go on to argue that *Kim* performs an analogous erasure of

[2] It is important to recognize that Indian nationalism was not, as has sometimes been argued, a de facto creation of British political and cultural practices in India. Moreover, the work of subalternist historians has taught us to be wary of accepting nationalist historiography, whose early spokespeople

Indian unrest.) In countering the unspoken claim of nationalists to a prior nation destroyed by the conquering power, Strachey cites Seeley's remark: 'India had no jealousy of the foreigner, because there was no India, and therefore, properly speaking, no foreigner' (qtd. in Strachey 1911: 6). Armed with this theory, Strachey asserts that despite the establishment of a central Government of India, 'the growth of a single Indian nationality is impossible' (7–8). Strachey's denial of national life to the entity called 'India', which, nevertheless, remains the title of his book, became the standard line of British turn-of-the-century writing about the subcontinent. Thus Valentine Chirol, dismissing the Congress in his well-known book of essays *Indian Unrest*, declares that 'a movement confined to a mere fraction of the population' has no right to be called national, 'even if the variegated jumble of races and peoples, castes and creeds that make up the population of India were not in itself an antithesis to all that the word "national" implies' (Chirol 1979: 6). For Charles Dilke, who observed 'how much our Government has done to create an India in the minds . . . of the most active and thoughtful among the small instructed minority of the peninsula', the supporters of the Congress movement overestimated 'the amount of unity which has been attained', and he insisted that India is 'a continent rather than a single country' (Dilke 1890: 403).

Although Dilke's argument is more sympathetic to Indian dissidence, provided this was coded within the language of 'loyal opposition', it contains the clearest statement of the problem with which Kipling wrestles in *Kim*. On detecting 'that glimmering of the idea of nationality that some find in India at the present time', he states, 'there can be no more urgent problem in connection with the Empire than that of tracing its extent and seeing how far we can meet or guide the movement' (406). In contrast to Strachey's logic of negation and denial, Dilke employs the language of negotiation, emphasizing the extent to which Indian nationalism has its roots in British policy: 'The tendency of our Government is necessarily in many matters to fuse India, and to cause a steady extension of that process of bringing the people of India together' (404). Nevertheless, Dilke too balks at the idea that specific British techniques of power will 'necessarily' lead to the construction of an Indian nation, a movement that might lie beyond 'our' abilities to 'meet or guide'; and although scornful of 'some

were British-educated, as the privileged narrative of the past and anticolonial resistance. See especially Guha (1992); see also Sarker (1973).

of the half informed' who believe that 'railway communication in itself' is putting an end to 'racial, religious, and linguistic differences in India' (404), he cites without dissent the preface to the report of 'one of the National Congresses' which 'frankly states that most of the delegates have to leave their homes to make long journeys into, to them, unknown provinces, inhabited by populations speaking unknown languages' (404–5).

Turning now to Kipling, I want to argue that *Kim* also recognizes the emerging idea of an Indian nation which is celebrated to the extent that it represents the arrival of 'modernity' – trains, 'efficient' bureaucratic government, the abolition of caste and religious differences – and disavowed in that it signals an anticolonial nationalism. Kipling's tableaux of Indian diversity on the train boarded by Kim and the Lama, a 'fat Hindu money-lender', an Amritsar prostitute, a Punjabi soldier, a wealthy Hindu couple, a Sikh artisan (Kipling 1987: 75–6), registers the process whereby modern railway communication means an end to caste-ridden distinctions, speeding India towards the day when everybody will be, as Kim says of himself and the lama – 'beyond all castes' (244). However, the novel also negates the possibility that such 'progress' might also lead to Indian resistance in the name of a secular nationalism. Thus the Western-educated British agent Hurree Chunder Mookerjee, who speaks in the accents of the comic 'babu', uses the language of Indian dissent in order to ingratiate himself with the French and Russian enemies of the Raj, thereby perverting and denying the impulses of an oppositional idiom devised by the Bengali upper-middle-class intelligentsia:

> He became thickly treasonous, and spoke in terms of sweeping indecency of a Government which had forced upon him a white man's education and neglected to supply him with a white man's salary. He babbled tales of oppression and wrong till the tears ran down his cheeks for the miseries of his land. . . . Never was so unfortunate a product of English rule in India more unhappily thrust upon aliens. (286)

Kim suppresses the threat represented by such opinions by making the latent meaning of Hurree's performance the exact opposite of its manifest content. Kipling's novel creates an implied reader who has absolutely no doubt that British rule in India is infinitely preferable to French or Russian rule, and who cannot even conceive of Indian self-government except, as here, as a form of comic relief from the side of

Hurree that is what Edward Said calls the 'ontologically funny native' (Said 1987: 33).

Nevertheless, despite this narrative confidence in the necessity of British rule, Kipling's actual, as opposed to his implied, readers, can discern the danger of Indian unrest, even as this is parodically trans-mitted by Hurree. Phillip Wegner has argued that 'the very narrative action of *Kim* represents a strategic attempt to *re-contain* those anxiety-producing conflicts that threaten British rule in India ... Kipling does not deny the existence of an anti-imperial presence, but rather engages in a careful *negation* of it' (Wegner 1993–94: 140; emphases in original). In Said's reading, the 'tendentious' logic by which Kipling refers to the rebellion of 1857 only via the loyal Indian army officer, 'whose much more likely nationalist counterpart . . . is never seen in the novel at all', serves to forestall the use of the sepoys' revolt in the discourse of contemporary Indian resistance. Moreover, the loyal old soldier rewarded for his assistance in putting down the 'madness' of 1854, and respected by the men on the spot, the district commissioners, acts to nullify the aims of both the mutineers and the proto-nationalists of the turn of the century. The unnamed soldier received a plot of land 'from the hands of the state – a free gift to me and mine' (101); he thus gets the land that the rebels had claimed for themselves. The prospect of nationalist Indians taking control of Indian land is hereby carefully contained and negated. In this Kipling has 'left the world of history, and entered the world of imperialist polemic' (Said 1987: 26).

This world is one of martial romance designed for those who nostalgically longed for more personal government in India and decried the proliferation of the modern, bureaucratic rule instituted after the rebellion. For example, the author of several articles on the Indian unrest in *Blackwood's Magazine* complained that district commissioners were becoming 'mere reporting machines' ('Adminis-tration' 1907: 151). 'Instead of being able to act, the man on the spot is too often obliged to sit down and write a report, . . . [even though] what the Eastern desires is personal government' (150–1). Kipling's novel, then, attempts to turn back the clock on the development of what C.A. Bayly calls Britain's 'empire of information' in India (Bayly 1996). Whereas the East India Company's spectacular conquest of India had been enabled by taking over and manipulating 'the sophisticated systems of internal espionage and political reporting which had long been deployed by the kingdoms of the Indian subcontinent' (Bayly 1996: 365), the new Government of India instituted more 'modern' forms of information and control, which, according to Bayley, left much of the country literally unknowable to the British administrators.

Kim registers a reaction against these administrative routines and an attempt to inject romance back into 'indigenous' forms of communication, especially spying. At the same time the novel works against the genre of romance by deploying the figure of the new 'reporting machine' in the service of India's government. Resisting, or perhaps doubting, its own logic of ceremonial power, the novel celebrates the modern forms of surveillance that included the collection and classification of reports, memoranda, academic papers, and other information that make up what Thomas Richards has called the 'imperial archive', and which Kipling calls the Great Game (Richards 1993). Romance – 'far and far into the Back of Beyond' – exists in tension with, and in the very same sentence as, the language of modern administration: Mahbub Ali, 'a wealthy and enterprising trader, whose caravans penetrated far and far into the Back of Beyond, was registered in one of the locked books of the Indian Survey Department as C25 1B' (69).

Kim is caught in a double bind: centralization of British rule along bureaucratic lines, employing a strict antinomy between Briton and Indian, threatens to produce the apparatuses of a future Indian nation-state, and must therefore be countered by a retreat into the world of close personal contact between British and 'natives'. Thus the Great Game, which appears to be ubiquitous, running 'like a shuttle throughout all Hind' (Kipling 1987: 273), must paradoxically *fail* to map the Indian nation it appears to control. For to fix permanently the borders of India, and to carry out the kind of detailed surveillance of towns and villages that Kim and Mahbub Ali engage in, would be to create a fully knowable, totally administered India. Such an entity could then bring the people of India together in a world 'beyond all castes', eliminating the rationale for British rule. While the lower level players in the Game, like Mahbub Ali and Kim, imagine its vast unity – ' "The Game is so large that one sees but a little at a time" ' (217) – Kipling intimates the possibility that the system ultimately fails to cohere, except insofar as it produces in its subjects the fantasy of its own omnipotence and omniscience, which is the strongest guarantee against future Mutiny-scale revolts.

We can see the novel struggling with this contradictory logic in the chapters where Lurgan warns Kim of the total control of information exercised by the Government of India, saying of someone who tried to sell state secrets in Simla, 'Perhaps if he were very clever, he might live out the day – but not the night' (208), an assurance countermanded by the narrator a few pages earlier, in terms taken both from the romance genre and ethnography:

> A man who knows his way there [in Simla] can defy all the police of India's summer capital, so cunningly does verandah communicate with verandah, alley-way with alley-way, and bolt-hole with bolt-hole . . . Here are discussed by courtesans the things which are supposed to be profoundest secrets of the India Council. (194)

Since the curious logic of the novel *requires* that secrets leak out of the imperial regime, Kipling shows the gaps and the instability within a system of which Kim becomes an integral part. Describing the results of a survey of the 'mysterious city of Bikanir', the archivist-narrator comments on inaccuracies and illegibility (218). There *must* be gaps and mistakes in the classification of this information, in the reduction of India to writing, in order that the novel can look back to the world of romance, and away from the emerging apparatus of the nation-state. Hence the boundaries of India must remain fluid and contested. The site of the greatest British anxiety in the late nineteenth century was the border between Punjab and Afghanistan, and its porousness, traversed by information and rival armies, sets the plot of *Kim* in motion. Seen as a possible route for a Russian invasion of India, it was also the setting for innumerable imperial romances of the Frontier, including Kipling's own 'The Ballad of East and West'. The novel begins with Kim carrying Mahbub Ali's message about 'five confederated Kings [on the Northwest Frontier], a Hindu banker in Peshawur, a firm of gun-makers in Belgium, and an important, semi-independent Mohammedan ruler to the south' (70). Kim's successful transmission of this intelligence to Creighton enables the mobilization of British troops; this in turn facilitates Kim's delivery into the hands of one of the regiments, the Mavericks, and the fulfilment of the prophecy of the red bull on the green field.

The instability of British India's borders allows for the deployment of both the romance genre and its apparent opposite, the new science of political geography (the Great Game is, after all, an offshoot of the India Survey). The unsuccessful attempt by the confederated kings to ambush 'the bullying, red-bearded horse-dealer [Mahbub Ali] whose caravans ploughed through their fastnesses belly-deep in snow' (69), develops the theme of imperial romance proposed by Lord Curzon, viceroy of India at the time *Kim* was published. In his Romanes Lecture at Oxford University shortly after his return to Britain in 1907, he celebrated the life of the frontiersman 'on the outskirts of Empire, where the machine is relatively impotent and the individual is strong'. These imperial heroes, however, are also described in strictly mechanical terms by Curzon as 'serious instruments of serious work' (Curzon 1907: 57–8). Kipling heeded Curzon's rallying cry and reinscribed its apparent contradiction. Thus Kim is situated as both the representative of the invincible spirit of the British race, and a figure for the scientific work of geography and mapping, essential in a world of unstable borders and superpower rivalries. In a lecture to the Royal Geographical Society in 1899, Thomas Holdich, a senior member of the India Survey, complained that politicians were making insufficient use of the new tools of the geographical science, since only 'complete mapping can give . . . that preliminary information' required at a time which has been 'well defined as the boundary-making era'. Waxing eloquent, he contemplated 'an endless vista of political geography . . . a vast area of new land and sea to be explored and developed . . . a vision of great burdens for the white man to take up in far-off regions, dim and indefinite as yet' (Holdich 1899: 466–7). The allusion to Kipling here is no accident: the fantasy of 'complete mapping' in Holdich's first sentence collapses before the endless vistas and great burdens of an Empire that must continue to expand in order that it not come to an end.

In *The Indian Borderland*, Holdich follows 350 pages describing frontier wars and surveys with a vision of unceasing movement where '[p]olicy does not seem quite equal to stopping the final ends of frontier evolution' (Holdich 1901: 370–1). The exasperated geographer finds himself employing the fluid language of his own science – swamps and overflows – to describe the political logic of imperialism, which, in its unstoppable 'evolution', 'had acquired the status almost of a fact of nature' (Said 1987: 10). Once again, science becomes romance.

This inability of the science of mapping to control the Empire's excesses is recreated in *Kim*, which defies its own inscriptions of geographical and surveillance technologies, by positing a more powerful and archaic narrative of Indian unrest. When the French and Russian surveyors/agents on the northern borders are finally defeated, Kim muses on the success of the mission undertaken in the Himalayan foothills:

> Here were the emissaries of the dread Power of the North . . .
> suddenly smitten helpless . . . Tonight they lay out somewhere below
> him, chartless, foodless, tentless, gunless . . . And this collapse of
> their Great Game . . . had come about through no craft of Hurree's
> or contrivance of Kim's, but simply, beautifully, and inevitably as
> the capture of Mahbub's *fakir*-friends by the zealous young police-
> man at Umballa. (297)

Against the logic of the Great Games, whose reports might create a map of all India, Kipling sets another logic, one that is 'simple, beautiful, and inevitable', and which seems to contain and ultimately control the world of eager policemen, international spies, and the chains and compasses of the India Survey. At the moment of Kim's true initiation into the Great Game, success comes not from skill or contrivances, but from a force beyond the realm of strategy: the force of coincidence and chance that is always the prerogative of the novelist of romance, the same force that put Kim in the path of the Mavericks, and thus on the road of the Great Game.

It is important, therefore, to note that the collapse of the French and Russian incursion actually comes about in the melee that follows the Russian's attack on the lama. For it is onto the lama's vision after immersion in the River of the Arrow that Kipling displaces the ability to map India completely, one that the Great Game can never achieve: 'At that point, exalted in contemplation, I saw all Hind, from Ceylon in the sea to the Hills . . . I saw them at one time and in one place; for they were within the Soul' (337). For Said, 'the lama's encyclopedic vision of freedom strikingly resembles Colonel Creighton's Indian Survey . . . [but] what might have been a positivistic inventory of places and peoples within the scope of British dominion has become, in the lama's generous inclusiveness, a redemptive and, for Kim's sake, a therapeutic vision' (Said 1987: 19). My contention, however, is that the lama's complete knowledge is beyond the disciplinary regimes of Creighton's survey, or of the railway lines that criss-cross India and enable the lama to complete his wanderings. Moreover, Kim's response to the lama's arrival at the river marking the end of his search is pure positivism, and hardly adequate for a *chela* witnessing his teacher's enlightenment: ' "*Allah kerim!* Oh, well that the Babu was by! Wast thou very wet?" ' (338). I see a parting of the ways at the end of the novel: the lama's inclusiveness allows the implied English reader to imagine all India, and from a position removed from Indian secular nationalism, since the lama's status as an 'Oriental' religious mystic who is not actually Indian, disassociates him from Indian unrest. Meanwhile, the lama's redemption frees Kim from the need to follow the Way and permits him to continue the Great Game. When the lama declares to Mahbub Ali that Kim ' "must go forth as a teacher" ', the horse-trader/spy replies, ' "Certainly he must go forth as a teacher. He is somewhat urgently needed as a scribe by the state, for instance" ' (334). The work of a reporting machine is apparently never done.

Although the novel ends in an apparently serene moment of

romance – '[The lama] crossed his hands on his lap and smiled, as a man may who has won salvation for himself and his beloved' (338) – the reader knows that the blessed ignorance of the lama serves to sanction the realist/archivist mode of the novel: ' "Let him be a teacher; let him be a scribe – what matter? He will have attained Freedom at the end. The rest is illusion" ' (334). The lama's funding of Kim's education at St Xavier's school assures the development of a British administrator who is neither the Oxford schoolboy fresh from England, nor the Western-educated Indian who transforms himself into the anti-British nationalist; while the lama's travels, following 'the traces of the Blessed Feet [of the Buddha] throughout all India' (213), perform the work of 'complete mapping' urged by Thomas Holdich. The novel thus enables the work of the imperial archive to proceed without risk of producing the nationalist threat to its own control of Indian space. Moreover, the curator of the Lahore Museum, whom the lama continues to visit, becomes the real archivist of India's mapping: 'The Curator has still in his possession a most marvellous account of [the lama's] wanderings and meditations' (213). It is this record, never divulged to the reader, which is the guarantee of continued British rule in India.

Richard Popplewell, in his book *Intelligence and Imperial Defence*, refers to the myth concocted in *Kim* 'of an all-seeing, far-sighted Raj' (Popplewell 1995: 30). I, however, have been arguing that in Kipling's vision of the Great Game, the Raj is constituted by its blindspots and failure to cohere into an organized whole. In the final section of this essay, I want to suggest that this construction of the Indian Empire as simultaneously far-reaching and also fragmentary and open to chance, takes Kipling's novel out of the geographical and historical realm of India that is its immediate setting, and situates it in the context of wider debates about the shape and future of the British Empire at the beginning of the twentieth century. Despite Kipling's elaboration of an intricate spy network in late nineteenth-century British India, historians disagree about the extent to which such an organization existed at that time. Popplewell claims that until Lord Curzon created the Department of Criminal Intelligence in 1903, there was no 'institutionalization and systematic use of political intelligence' (Popplewell 1995: 14) – nor was this new department all-seeing and far-sighted, since it paid no attention to the Indian National Congress (Popplewell, 1995: 44–5). By contrast, Bayly emphasizes the extensive networks of spies and informers on which the British relied to maintain their power, both before and after 1857 (Bayly 1996: 339). These assertions are not necessarily incompatible, and Bayly traces the ways in which the

British developed centralized, all-India forms of communication and surveillance, while relegating to the local level the use of spies and more informal techniques of surveillance and policing.

As Bayly puts it, albeit within a binary opposition between 'modern'-Western and 'traditional'-Indian that I find troubling, 'What emerged [after 1857] was a dual economy of knowledge: an "advanced" sector, which used western forms of representation and communication subsisting within an attenuated but still massive hinterland employing older styles of information and debate' (Bayly 1996: 372). The question then becomes: where does *Kim* turn in its attempt to join these two 'economies of knowledge', one centralized and 'modern', the other diffused and 'native'? The beginnings of an answer are to be found in Popplewell's parenthetical observation that, in contrast to India itself, '[o]ne area where the British had regularly used spies was Ireland, where unrest was always on the cards. Undoubtedly espionage played an effective and continuous role there in maintaining British domination' (34). Kim, of course, is Irish by birth, and it is to Ireland, and the contradictory place of the Irish in the British Empire at the turn of the century, that we can look for one explanation of the novel's structure.

S.B. Cook, in his work on affinities between India and Ireland in the nineteenth century, notes that the British developed a national educa-tion system and a national police force in Ireland well before such centralization was deemed necessary in Britain itself (Cook 1993: 19), and certainly well before the unifying policies of Lord Curzon's regime in India. It has now become commonplace for historians to refer to the 'Irish model' of colonial policing, which culminated in the 1907 decision that all British colonial police officers were to undergo initial training at the headquarters of the Royal Irish Constabulary in Dublin. Unlike the British domestic police forces, the Irish police were centrally controlled, armed, and organized along quasi-military lines (Jeffery 1996b: 10). Thus while some recent work questions the degree of similarity between Irish policing and other, very different, colonial situations (e.g. Hawkins 1991), it is clear that Kipling borrowed from an Irish model in developing his vision of a centralized secret police in *Kim*.[3]

Without suggesting that the India of *Kim* is a displaced version of Ireland, I am arguing for the significance of Kim's Irishness. Irish soldiers were present in disproportionate numbers in the Indian and indeed the imperial army throughout the nineteenth century: between

[3] In what follows, I am indebted to the work of Amy Martin. See also T.G. Fraser, 'Ireland and India'.

1825 and 1850, half of all white recruits to the Bengal army were Irish, although the numbers declined in the second half of the century (Jeffery 1996c: 94–5). For his entire writing career, but particularly in his Indian stories, Kipling celebrates the role of these Irish recruits, and their unswerving loyalty to the Empire. This coexisted with a near-fanatical opposition to Irish Home Rule. In 1912, when loyalist politicians in Ulster were beginning to talk openly of armed resistance to Home Rule, Kipling apparently offered £30,000 to the Unionist cause (Powell 1996: 146); and in a letter of December 1913 to his friend H.A. Gwynne, he wrote: 'You aren't watching a skirmish of politicians . . . you are watching the revolt of the [Unionist] Irish . . . Our game is organised resistance *to the end'* (qtd. in Lowry 1996: 192; emphasis in original). In 1923, Kipling edited a two-volume collection of the letters, diaries, and songs of the Irish Guards regiment in World War I, the regiment of his son, John, who was killed at the Battle of Loos in 1915. The introduction suggests Kipling's attitude to loyal Irish soldiers:

> They were in no sense any man's command. They needed minute comprehension, quick sympathy and inflexible justice, which they repaid by individual devotion and a collective good-will . . . The discipline of the Guards, demanding the utmost that can be exacted of the men, requires of the officer unresting care of his men under all conditions. (Kipling 1923: xiii)

Appropriately enough, the Irish Guards were formed to reward the bravery of Irish soldiers who fought to preserve the integrity of the Empire during the Anglo-Boer War, with Field Marshall Lord Wolseley, the Irish-born commander-in-chief of the British Army, declaring that: 'The Queen's appreciation of the gallant services rendered by her Irish soldiers will have a magical effect upon that sentimental and imaginative race all over the world' (qtd. in Jeffery 1996c: 96). By paying homage to the loyal, martial spirit of 'Celtic psychology', both Kipling and Wolseley sought to bind Ireland and the Irish more firmly to Britain and the Empire.

In this period, however, Irish unrest paralleled Indian unrest, and taken together, they formed a powerful threat to the Empire. Throughout the second half of the nineteenth century there was concern that Fenian sympathizers were infiltrating Irish regiments of the British army, including the army in India, a concern that was not without foundation. The earliest historian of the movement, John Devoy, claimed that there were 1,600 sworn members of the Irish Revolutionary Brotherhood in the

Dublin garrison of the British Army in 1865 (Newsinger 1994: 40–1); and James Stephens, the founder of the IRB, thought that there were some 15,000 Fenians serving in the British army.[4] Although the Fenian movement was obviously anathema to Kipling, he was attracted by at that time the idea of an oath-bound secret society, in which, theoretically at least, those at the centre of the movement, designated by the letter A, commanded, and knew the identities of, only nine 'B's, or captains, who in turn each passed on orders to nine 'C's, or sergeants (Newsinger 1994: 25). This model is echoed in the code numbers of the agents of the Great Game in *Kim*: Mahbub Ali is C25 (whose statements are checked against the stories of R17 and M4); the man who Kim aids on the train by disguising him as a *saddhu* is known only as E23.

By mimicking the structure of a 'terrorist' organization in the service of the Raj, Kipling could be said to be simultaneously representing and containing an Irish rebellion in which both proponents and opponents of Indian nationalism found an easy analogy. S.B. Cook notes how nineteenth-century British observers and officials chronicled similarities such as: 'impoverished populations, religious pluralism, sectarian division and strife, social domination by "meddlesome priests", peasant economies, traditional village communities, pre-modern cultures and recent and not altogether uneventful experiences of British rule' (Cook 1993: 29–30). In 1880, Lord Dufferin, the Anglo-Irish viceroy of India, complained of 'the importation en bloc from England, or rather from Ireland, of the perfected machinery of modern democratic agitation', also communicating his anxiety to the secretary of state for India: 'Unless some definite line is taken . . . we shall soon have something like a Home Rule organization established in India, on Irish lines, under the patronage of Irish and Radical members of Parliament' (qtd. in Fraser 1996: 87). Such comparisons between India and Ireland were also made by British writers on both sides of the debate: *Blackwood's Magazine* claimed that '[o]nly the hysterical imagination of a Bengali or an Irish Nationalist could have made a tragic grievance' of the partition of Bengal in 1905, since this was merely an administrative necessity ('Treatment of Sedition' 1907: 257). By contrast, the Labour leader Keir Hardie, during his tour of the areas of East Bengal where the

---

[4] For the most part, Irish regiments in the British Army did not rebel against their officers, although there is one famous exception: the mutiny of the Connaught Rangers in the Punjab in June–July 1920. Three hundred soldiers declared then that they 'would do no more work until the British troops had been removed from Ireland' (qtd. in Jeffery 1996c: 116). The mutiny did not spread to other regiments and was quickly crushed (see Jeffery 1996c: 116–18).

swadeshi movement was at its height, witnessed Indian policemen setting up a shop to sell the foreign-made goods that were being boycotted: 'I question whether even in Ireland, of which India constantly reminded me, an instance of the public authorities acting in this fashion could be found?' (Hardie 1909: 26). Kipling drew on this tradition of likening India and Ireland, and because his concern was with the threats to British power posed by nationalists and rebels in both countries, he negotiated the problems raised by Indian and Irish unrest by representing their forms and reversing their import (as in the secret code names in *Kim*), in the interest of achieving a higher unity for that fragile entity, the British Empire.

This configuring of Irish and Indian discontent is evident in Kipling's story 'The Mutiny of the Mavericks' (included in the collection *Life's Handicap*). The story begins in the strongholds of the Fenians within the émigré Irish communities of the United States. Using and parodying the cell structure of the IRB, Kipling's narrator recounts the tale of how 'the Third Three of the I.A.A.', under orders from the First Three in New York, decide to send the *agent provocateur* Mulcahy to infiltrate the Mavericks regiment in India – the same, fictional, regiment in which Kim's Irish father served in and from which he deserted. The aim of this mission is not merely freedom for Ireland, but destabilizing 'the British Empire and all that lay therein' (Kipling n.d.: 59) – a 'cursed empire' prone to 'blunders'. This gives Kipling the opportunity to remark on the ineptitude of the imperial ruling class, because for him the security of the Empire lies with its (Irish) footsoldiers, who obey orders but ultimately know more of India than do their officers and the government. Because the narrator concedes that trying to undermine British confidence in its army is the correct strategy for the IAA, this allows Kipling to disturb the complacency of a reading public assured of the Empire's continuity and stability, while rebuilding confidence on firmer ground. When Mulcahy preaches conspiracy among the Mavericks, they consume the quantities of beer his mother sends from New York and pretend to complicity with his mutinous plans. Here Kipling mobilizes a tired stereotype of the drunken Irish, while also intimating that the soldiers loved the game for its own sake. The twist in the story comes at the end, when the Mavericks, just as in *Kim*, are posted to the Northwest frontier to fight 'the annual little war on the border' (67). The tension that lies behind Kipling's comedy, the anxiety about regiments in open revolt, comes to the surface here. In battle against the Afghans, the Mavericks steel themselves by singing the song heralding 'the general rising of

Erin' taught them 'in the strictest confidence' by the IAA agent (74). This inspires the whole regiment, but especially Mulcahy, to unheard of feats of bravery, and the Fenian rebel dies a noble, loyal death leading the final charge on the Afghan positions.

Just as *Kim* employs, and transfers to India, both the apparatus of British political intelligence in Ireland and the cell structure of the IRB, so 'The Mutiny of the Mavericks' ultimately appropriates Irish resistance to the service of the British cause. Kipling raises the spectre of Irish rebellion allied to Indian resistance – Mulcahy's plan according to one soldier is that ' "We're to join with the niggers, and look for help from Dhulip Singh [the disloyal 'Maharaja of the Punjab'] and the Russians!" ' (64) – and then defuses it, for the regiment would afterwards become a force for the perpetuation of the Empire. Although less rewarding than *Kim*, the tale does shed light on the strategic aims of the more complex text. Kim's hybridity, simultaneously Indian, Irish, and English, crystallizes Kipling's response to the dangers threatening British rule in India and the wider Empire: the hybrid Irish, who are both colonizers and colonized, and thus 'maverick', will defend the borders of the Empire at the same time as they challenge its integrity and must themselves be contained. This ambivalence is expressed in Kim's membership of the secret society, the Sons of the Charm, invented by Hurree (231). In his essay 'Ethnography and the Hybrid Boy', Don Randall suggests that Hurree has thus established a secret network within the Great Game, which escapes the attention of Colonel Creighton and the all-seeing Raj (Randall 1996: 90). Read in this way, the Sons of the Charm are a dissident organization led by Bengali nationalists (Hurree) and Irish radicals (Kim); yet it could also be understood as simply another subset of the Great Game, in which even agents working independently function ultimately in the service of the state. Once again, Kipling combines both the surveillance networks and the secret societies in his elaboration of the Great Game, coopting Indian and Irish resistance for the greater good of the Empire.

It is specifically Kim's Irishness that allows him to be a 'native' without being Indian, and to be a 'Sahib' without being English. Poised between these poles, Kim can be both rebel and governor at the same time, as is the title character of another early Indian story, 'Namgay Doola'. Here the English narrator divines the Irish roots of the red-haired Namgay, a tireless worker but also an instinctual rebel against the regime of a Himalayan principality. The final clue to Namgay's ancestry is his garbled, creole version of 'The Wearing of the

Green', prompting the narrator to advise the king that the unruly Irishman be put in charge of the militia force: ' "Give him honour as may befall and full allowance of work, but look to it, oh, king, that neither he nor his [family] hold a foot of earth from thee henceforward" ' (Kipling n.d.: 38).[5]

Collapsing the figures of the rebel and the ruler into the hybrid Irish finesses some of the problems facing British writers on India at the turn of the century: the emergence of a British-educated Indian elite with proto-nationalist tendencies; the desire to maintain full British control over all aspects of the administration versus recognizing the need to include Indians in the running of their own affairs; the necessity for a modern, centralized bureaucracy, versus the benefits of quasi-feudal local structures of power. However, while Kim's Irishness is a way of containing these problems by joining Irish and Indian dissent, it also suggests the possibility of a broader threat to the Empire. Certainly Kipling's contemporary readers understood *Kim* as a response to a set of crises, both 'domestic' and 'imperial'. The anonymous *Blackwood's* reviewer ended his praise of the novel thus:

> We may not leave Mr Kipling's book without brief reference to the sense of exhilaration with which it cannot but be read by all Britons who are lovers of their country . . . To the despicable minority of our countrymen who invariably lavish their sympathy and support upon the king's enemies, the whole tone of the work will be as gall and wormwood. Mr Kipling lifts the veil, and reveals a wheel or two of the machinery at work night and day for the preservation of our Indian Empire. ('Recent Fiction' 1901: 795)

If the Empire needs to be preserved, then the assumption is that it is under threat from the king's numerous enemies. Kipling's work represents an attempt to mediate this imperial crisis: on the one hand, proposing a new fictive unity for the Empire, one that includes even the king's rebel subjects, and on the other hand, glimpsing the fact that, dialectically speaking, providing the Empire with the illusion of coherence and functional unity accelerates the pace at which the Empire helps to produce its own demise.

---

[5] The narrator eventually translates the song as 'They're hanging men and women, too,/ For the wearing of the green' (Kipling n.d.: 36).

Works Cited

'The Administration of India', 1907. *Blackwood's Magazine* 182 (July–Dec.), 147–51.

Bayly, C.A., 1996. *Empire and Information: Intelligence Gathering and Social Communication in India, 1780–1870*, Cambridge: Cambridge UP.

Booker, M. Keith, 1997. *Colonial Power, Colonial Texts: India in the Modern British Novel*, Ann Arbor: U of Michigan P.

Chaudhuri, Nirad C., 1957. 'The Finest Story about India in English', *Encounter* 8 (April), 47–53.

Chirol, Valentine, 1979. *Indian Unrest* (orig. pub. 1910), New Delhi: Light & Life.

Cook, S.B., 1993. *Imperial Affinities: Nineteenth-Century Analogies and Exchanges Between India and Ireland*, New Delhi: Sage.

Curzon, George Nathaniel, 1907. *Frontiers*, Oxford: Clarendon P.

Dilke, Charles Wentworth, 1890. *Problems of Greater Britain*, London: Macmillan.

Fraser, T.G., 1996. 'Ireland and India', in Jeffery 1996a, 77–93.

Guha, Ranajit, 1988. 'The Prose of Counter-Insurgency', in *Selected Subaltern Studies*, ed. Guha and Gayatri Chakravorty Spivak, New York: Oxford UP.

——, 1992. 'Dominance without Hegemony and its Historiography', in *Subaltern Studies VI: Writings on South Asian History and Society*, ed. Guha, New Delhi: Oxford UP, 210–309.

Hardie, J. Keir, 1909. *India: Impressions and Suggestions*, New York: B.W. Huebsch.

Hawkins, Richard, 1991. 'The "Irish Model" and the Empire: A Case for Reassessment', in *Policing the Empire: Government, Authority and Control, 1830–1940*, ed. David M. Anderson and David Killingray, Manchester: Manchester UP.

Holdich, Thomas H., 1899. 'The Use of Practical Geography Illustrated by Recent Frontier Operations', *Geographical Journal* 13 (Jan.–June), 465–80.

——, 1901. *The Indian Borderland: 1880–1900*, London: Methuen.

'India 1857–1907: Retrospect and Prospect', 1907. *Blackwood's Magazine* 181 (Jan.–June), 611–19.

Jeffery, Keith, ed., 1996a. *An Irish Empire? Aspects of Ireland and the British Empire*, Manchester: Manchester UP.

——, 1996b. 'Introduction', in Jeffery 1996a, 1–24.

——, 1996c. 'The Irish Military Tradition and the British Empire', in Jeffery 1996a, 94–122.

Kipling, Rudyard, 1923. *The Irish Guards in the Great War, Part I*, The Writings in Prose and Verse of Rudyard Kipling, Vol. 29, New York: Scribner's.

——, 1987. *Kim* (orig. pub. 1901), ed. Edward W. Said, London: Penguin.

——, n.d. *Selected Works of Rudyard Kipling*, Vol. 3, New York: P.F. Collier.

Lowry, Donal, 1996. 'Ulster Resistance and Loyalist Rebellion in the Empire', in Jeffery 1996a, 191–215.

Nair, Rukmini Bhaya, 1995. 'The Pedigree of the White Stallion: Postcoloniality and Literary History', in *The Uses of Literary History*, ed. Marshall Brown, Durham, NC: Duke UP, 159–86.

Newsinger, John, 1994. *Fenianism in Mid-Victorian Britain*, London: Pluto.

Parry, Benita, 1972. *Delusions and Discoveries: Studies on India in the British Imagination, 1880–1930*, Berkeley: U of California P.

Popplewell, Richard J., 1995. *Intelligence and Imperial Defence: British Intelligence and the Defence of the Indian Empire, 1904–1924*, London: Frank Cass.

Randall, Don, 1996. 'Ethnography and the Hybrid Boy in Rudyard Kipling's *Kim*', *ARIEL: A Review of International English Literature* 27:3, 79–104.

'Recent Fiction', 1901. *Blackwood's Magazine* 170 (July–Dec.), 793–806.

Richards, Thomas, 1993. *The Imperial Archive: Knowledge and the Fantasy of Empire*, London: Verso.

Said, Edward W., 1987. 'Introduction', in *Kim*, by Rudyard Kipling. London: Penguin.

Seeley, John, 1972. *The Expansion of England* (orig. pub. 1883), ed. John Gross, Chicago: U of Chicago P.

Stokes, Eric, 1959. *The English Utilitarians and India*, Oxford: Oxford UP.

Strachey, John [Sr.], 1911. *India: Its Administration and Progress*, 4th ed., London: Macmillan.

'The Treatment of Sedition in India', 1907. *Blackwood's Magazine* 181 (Jan.–June), 257–65.

Wegner, Phillip E., 1993–94. ' "Life as he would have it": The Invention of India in Kipling's *Kim*', *Cultural Critique* 26, 129–60.

Williams, Patrick, 1994. '*Kim* and Orientalism', in *Colonial Discourse and Post-Colonial Theory: A Reader*, ed. Laura Chrisman and Williams, New York: Columbia UP, 480–97.

Wilson, Edmund, 1941. 'The Kipling that Nobody Read', in *The Wound and the Bow*, Boston: Houghton Mifflin.

The Canker of Empire: Colonialism, Autobiography and the Representation of Illness: Jack London and Robert Louis Stevenson in the Marquesas

LAWRENCE PHILLIPS

Insidious Questions: When we are confronted with any manifestation which someone has permitted us to see, we may ask: what is it meant to conceal? What is it meant to draw our attention from? What prejudice does it seek to raise? And again, how far does the subtlety of dissimulation go? And in what respect is the man mistaken? (Nietzsche, *The Dawn of the Day*, section 523)

WHILST MUCH WORK has been done on the relationship between late nineteenth-century gothic literature and imperial anxieties,[1] a seldom explored characteristic of colonial literature is its obsession with illness. The association is clear in such gothic tales as Bram Stoker's *Dracula*, whose physical appearance and sexual overtones are reminiscent of the common myth of the consumptive's over-heated libido. Dracula's physical locale – the east – not only links this 'diseased' individual and those he infects with xenophobia and racism, but also reveals a deep unease over the changing status of Britain's empire, 'becoming a parasitic rather than a competitive economy, living off the remains of world monopoly' (Hobsbawm 1969: 192). Yet one might also note the prominent use of illness in both Conrad's *Heart of Darkness* and Rider Haggard's *King Solomon's Mines*, where the ultimate quest object is the recovery of a diseased white man – or in Kipling's *Kim*, where the hero must throw off a debilitating fever which attests to the vitality of his white blood. However, behind such metaphoric uses of illness and disease lies the reality encountered by Europeans of the effects of unfamiliar climate and new diseases. More devastating and insidious were the epidemics of European transmitted diseases among indigenous

---

[1] See Patrick Bratlinger's, *Rule of Darkness: British Literature and Imperialism 1830–1914* (Ithaca: Cornell University Press, 1988); Daniel Pick's, *Faces of Degeneration: A European Disorder c.1848–c.1918* (Cambridge: Cambridge University Press, 1989); and H.L. Malchow's *Gothic Images of Race in Nineteenth-Century England* (Stanford: Stanford University Press, 1996).

peoples. Thence illness and disease in turn of the century colonial writing represents a complex intersection of the material consequences of colonialism with displaced psychological unease and racial stereotypes.

In his recent study – *Representing the South Pacific: Colonial Discourse from Cook to Gauguin* – Rod Edmond explores the prevalence of metaphors of illness in the colonial South Pacific, focusing primarily on Jack London's journalism and fiction in and of the Hawaiian and Marquesan groups. Edmond's analysis relies heavily on the metaphorical alignment he detects between contagion and the effects of colonialism, which he sees reflected in the physical debilitation of the colonised: 'And the disease had rich metaphorical possibilities not only as a way of expressing the innate corruption of indigenous cultures, but also for describing the damaging effects of imperialism itself' (Edmond 1997: 197). In this passage Edmond refers specifically to leprosy, but his comment is equally applicable to the broader point he makes about the dynamics involved in such metaphors. On the one hand, there is a colonial discourse which constructs Western contact as a beneficial, civilising process, bringing the ubiquitous degenerate 'native' to god, technological progress and global capitalism. And on the other hand is a counter-discourse of the 'contaminating power of European civilisation' (Ibid.: 194) which robs the same 'native' of his/her culture, land and political determination. Although Edmond does not make the point explicitly himself, this barely surpressed duplicity, or perhaps culpability, generates a need in colonial discourse to displace feelings of guilt whilst promoting the supposed 'benefits' of colonialism.

Whilst not necessarily dissenting from Edmond's general thesis, I wish to examine a little more closely metaphors of illness as a reflection of individual conscience, experience and memory – an autobiographical mode – in conjunction with material reality and internalised imperial ideologies. This process is largely taken for granted by Edmond who remains content to trace the interplay between Western anxieties over the material and cultural consequences of colonialism and the overarching sense of European superiority. He does not question how these processes reveal the contradictory relationship of autobiographical self-fashioning and experiential reality as it is subtly shaped by colonial discourse.

My reservations about Edmond's conceptualisation stem from the way it endorses a symbiotic relationship between guilt and justification. By omitting to consider how this relationship may in fact serve to strengthen colonial discourse and practice, he is at risk of participating in that process. Not altogether unaware that this risk exists, he attempts to destabilise it ideologically by locating critical closure in the personal travails of the writer he is examining – the Pacific voyages and tropical illnesses of Jack London in his chapter on disease and colonialism:

> The same instability of human tissue was written all over London's body by the time he abandoned the cruise of the *Snark* . . . His own body had become the site on which the metaphors of disease and corruption that he had used to express the effects of Western settlement were literalised. (Edmond 1997: 211)

In effect, the material body has become reduced by Edmond to an expression of metaphoricity; the illness metaphor is seen to be materially realised through London's body. This conceptual absurdity can only be sustained if metaphor is cut asunder from its material basis, i.e. the dialectical process whereby autobiographical writing mediates between lived experience and the metaphors which order experience and memory.

One of the reasons that Edmond falls into this discursive trap is his uncritical adoption of Susan Sontag's analysis of metaphors of Illness. To understand why this is so we need to look at Sontag's analysis in *Illness as Metaphor* a little more closely: 'it is hardly possible to take up residence in the kingdom of the ill unprejudiced by the lurid metaphors with which it has been landscaped' (Sontag 1983: 7). Sontag's project, therefore, is to expose such metaphors to scrutiny and alleviate the ill from the 'putative or sentimental fantasies' such preconceptions entail (Ibid.). Yet, perceptive as her study is, it is difficult to throw off the suspicion that the simplification that metaphors obscure the truth is reductive and itself serves to obscure a complex dialectic. Metaphors of illness mediate between the experiential (actual illness), cultural preconceptions, personal sympathies and self-conceptualisation.

Moreover, she seems to suggest that 'metaphors' of illness have somehow become more 'real' than disease itself, or at least real enough to entirely obscure material reality which requires that they be discursively scraped off. I am not trying to say that the stigma that has grown up around certain illnesses does not exist, but metaphors are not simply curtains that can be drawn aside to reveal an obscured truth: they are sites of discursive interchange where contradictions are not resolved, but brought into an uneasy relationship. A failure to recognise this complexity reproduces a binary opposition between true and false which does nothing to assist our understanding of the fear that generated the image in the first place, nor the social, personal, political and cultural processes which create this antagonistic energy. The type of dialectical relationship I am proposing here 'does not simply separate things as conceptual opposites, for the essence of the process is that the opposites are in an active relationship of mutual contradiction' (Murphy 1972: 121).

Illness is a state which, literally and figuratively, cannot be amputated from physical being, social meaning, or figurative extrapolation. As Northrop Frye observes:

> Metaphor, then, arises in a state of society in which a split between a perceiving subject and perceived object is not yet habitual, and what it does in that context is to open up a channel or current of energy between human and natural worlds. (Frye 1991: 111)

Illness is a natural 'fact' which has a social meaning. Because of this, it is also an anchor on which cultural processes are affixed. Yet its manifestation is always uniquely devastating and personal. It can never become wholly abstract and habitualised.

I am not seeking to assert some naive unification of word and thing, yet I do wish counter the trend to deny all referentiality of the 'text' to an experiential reality. To do so, especially when writing of the brutal praxis of colonialism as I do here, leads to a discursive practice which reduces an all too real oppression to a question of rhetoric.[2] Edmond is not guilty of such reductionism. But by seeking to find a discursive closure in the details of London's own illnesses he ignores the fact that London's autobiographical self-representation is also a component of an ongoing dialectical process. It is neither an end in itself, nor subservient to the metaphors through which it operates. 'Experience', writes Jacques Derrida, 'lives and proclaims itself as the exclusion of writing, that is to say of the invoking of an "exterior", "sensible", "spatial" signifier interrupting self-presence' (qtd. by Silverman 1994). This view, I would argue, is manifestly challenged by the lived experience of illness, colonialism and their associated metaphors. Such binary separation between experience and writing is akin to Sontag's urge to cut through to an absolute truth, or Edmond's

---

[2] For a discussion of this practice, see my 'Lost in Space: Siting/Citing the In-Between of Homi Bhabha's *The Location of Culture*', in *Scrutiny2* Vol. 3 No. 1 (April 1998).

appropriation of London's self-presentation as some kind of metaphor for the metaphorisation of illness which is, in turn, a metaphor of colonialism.

My argument is that experiential reality is the outcome of a dialectical process in which discursive formulations interact with a seemingly chaotic sensual reality to produce experience. This process generates textual order and thence meaning(s) through the 'energy' of metaphor. Through an analysis of metaphors of disease and illness in both Robert Louis Stevenson's and Jack London's commentary on the Marquesas from *In The South Seas* and *The Cruise of the Snark* respectively,[3] this paper will suggest how the dialectic between the experiential reality and discursive formulation of the colonial Pacific, between autobiographical reflection and fictional representation might be read, so that the connection between materiality, memory and discourse can be mapped. London's and Stevenson's oeuvre are particularly well suited to this project, since they offer an abundance of autobiographical travel notes, diaries, and letters recording their respective residences in the Pacific Islands which inspired their fiction. The autobiographical nature of this material is essential to such an analysis, since it provides the textual connection between experiential reality and metaphor. As James Olney suggests, autobiography is the metaphorical ordering of memory and experience (Olney 1981: 3–50), which is akin to Stevenson's own view of the relationship between literature and life: 'Life is monstrous, infinite, illogical, abrupt and poignant; a work of art, in comparison, is neat, finite, self-contained, rational, flowing and emasculate' (McLynn 1993: 243). Thence the autobiographical trace within a text carries with it the referential quality of experiential reality, yet at the same time it is inseparable from the process that governs its figuration: discourse.

Stevenson's decision to travel in the South Pacific was conditioned both by a search for a favourable climate for his health, and a seemingly congenital inability to settle in one place. Prior to his departure for Hawaii on the yacht *Casco* early on the morning of 28 June 1888, his journeying had taken him to England, France, Italy, and Switzerland, as well as Germany and Austria in his youth. In 1879–80 he spent a year in San Francisco where he married his wife, Fanny Osbourne. Whilst such travels may not seem prodigious from a modern or, indeed, a late

---

[3] Robert Louis Stevenson, *In the South Seas* (London: William Heinemann, 1924) and Jack London, *The Cruise of the Snark* (London: Seafarer Books, 1971). Subsequent page references are to these editions.

nineteenth-century perspective, even in Britain Stevenson's life was marked by constant movement once he had left his parents house for good. Only in 1884 did Stevenson and Fanny settle in Bournemouth, which suited Fanny but where Stevenson was restless and dogged by ill-health. In 1888, following the death of his father, he inherited a considerable sum which provided the financial independence for travel. Armed with medical justification – probably contrived (see McLynn 1993: 277) – Stevenson, still dogged by poor health, was anxious to be on the move again. Lloyd Osbourne, his stepson recorded he was 'cheerful, even jubilant . . . He was plainly glad to be off, and the sooner the better' (qtd. in McLynn 1993: 277). Yet by the time Stevenson wrote the first lines of his account of his travels in the South Seas, this sense of elation and nervous energy unleashed had, it seems, been lost:

> For nearly ten years my health had been declining; and for some time before I set forth on my voyage, I believed I was come to the afterpiece of life, and had only the nurse and the undertaker to expect. It was suggested that I should try the south seas; and I was not unwilling to visit like a ghost, and be carried like a bale, among scenes that had attracted me in youth and health. (3)

Jack London is publicly celebrated as a wanderer. Aged only seventeen he shipped before the mast on the whaler the *Sophia Sutherland* for the sealing grounds off Japan. The following year, still only eighteen, he had joined Coxey's Army, part of a broader labour protest originating in various sections of the US which, in 1894, organised a number of marching 'armies' of the unemployed across America to converge on Washington. London's own journey originated in San Francisco although he deserted at Hannibal, Missouri. What followed was a period as a 'professional' hobo which he was later to record in *The Road*. In 1897, London joined the Klondike gold rush and departed for the Yukon that autumn. By 1902, now established as a writer, he was in London incognito gathering material in the city's slums for *The People of the Abyss*. By 1906, a successful, wealthy author and another restless spirit, London conceived of the idea to sail around the world and began to oversee the construction of his own yacht for the purpose: the *Snark*. First port of call would be Hawaii, but he would then consciously follow in Stevenson's wake to the Marquesas and later Samoa. The prospect of the journey filled him with as much jubilation as Stevenson, but in the forward to the collected essays written during the voyage – *The Cruise of the Snark* – he strikes a very different tone:

> Life that lives is life successful, and success is the breath of its nostrils. The achievement of a difficult feat is successful adjustment to a sternly exacting environment . . . Here is the sea, the wind, and the wave. Here are the seas, the winds, and the waves of the all the world. Here is a ferocious environment. And here is difficult adjustment, the achievement of which is delight to the small quivering vanity that is I. I like. I am so made. It is my own particular form of vanity, that is all. (5–7)

These two passages are strikingly at odds in terms of tone. Indeed, it is tempting to succumb to the common perception of these two authors: London, the quintessential man of action; a chronicler of humanity's battle with a savage nature. A Nietzchean overman incarnate. Stevenson, the gentle, rather saintly consumptive invalid; the writer of romantic adventure stories. The myths that have enveloped both authors could not present a greater contrast, engendered partly from popular readings of their most famous fiction and the careful post mortem media manipulation by their surviving spouses. Yet as we have already seen, they shared a common restlessness and aesthetically rather more. Frank McLynn cites London as Stevenson's 'true spiritual heir' (McLynn 1993: 157) and Charmian records London beside Stevenson's grave at Vailima remarking in a subdued voice: 'I wouldn't have gone out of my way to visit the grave of any other man in the world' (Charmian London n.d.: 19).

Yet a common restlessness and an aesthetic affinity makes the contrast between these two passages all the more marked. That they were both written post facto provides a clue.[4] Their respective state of health, another. Stevenson suffered from a number of debilitating illnesses during his life, although the most recurrent was a lung complaint whose symptoms included haemorrhages – dubbed 'Bluidy Jack' by Stevenson – assumed to be consumption (tuberculosis) although its exact nature was, and is, open to some speculation (McLynn 1993: 171–2). Residence in the South Pacific (particularly in Samoa) improved his condition considerably. As he wrote to Henry James: 'The sea, islands, the islanders, the island life and climate, make

---

[4] Whilst the essays comprising *The Cruise of the Snark* were written during the cruise itself for serial newspaper publication, the foreword where we find this passage was written after the return to California.

and keep me truly happier. These last two years I have been much at sea, and have never wearied; sometimes I have indeed grown impatient for some destination; more often I was sorry that the voyage drew so early to an end' (qtd. in Knight 1986: 185).

By contrast, cruising in the South Seas for Jack London brought progressive illness. By the time the yacht reached the Solomon Islands, it resembled a 'floating infirmary' including 'Solomon sores' or Yaws, 'raspberry-like skin eruptions and destructive lesions caused by a tropical spirochete' and a mysterious 'sun sickness' which impaired London's co-ordination, caused his hands to swell up and his skin to flake off (Lundquist 1987: 60). London had up to eight of these lesions at a time and writes with a strained light heatedness of his attempt to doctor them himself in the final chapter of *The Cruise of the Snark* entitled 'The Amateur M. D.' For once the iron constitution on which he had always relied was failing him: 'I was puzzled and frightened. All my life my skin had been famous for its healing powers, yet here was something that would not heal. Instead, it was daily eating up more skin, while it had eaten down clear through the skin and was eating up muscle itself' (315).

London was finally driven to consult doctors in Sydney, and the cruise was never resumed; it petered out in the glare of the Pacific sun and gnawing Pacific diseases. The death of Peggy their pet dog at what was to become the end of the cruise, greatly upset both Jack and Charmian. In her memoirs – *A Woman Among the Head Hunters* – the despair over the failure of their ambitions due to illness becomes entwined with their grief over the loss of the dog in a way that is clearly emblematic of a greater loss; the passing of the optimism and, perhaps, hubris, with which the cruise began: 'I know, Jack Knows . . . she was asking for him, for me, some word, some message, trying at the end of her blameless days, to pass across all space and difference of kind, her deathless faith' (Charmian London n.d.: 251). The loss of faith in self, human will and the superiority of the 'white man', perhaps, all undermined by illness.

Despite his celebration of the power of the human will in the forward to *The Cruise of the Snark*, it is the very defeat of the will by nature (illness and disease) that most accurately characterises London's experience. The pessimism of Stevenson's passage seems equally misplaced. Rather than some ghastly waif of his former self on the threshold of death, Stevenson gained strength and enjoyed considerable vitality in the Pacific, evidenced by a remarkable literary output, considerable sea voyages, the establishment of a home and plantation and a controversial involvement in Samoan politics. Whilst the autobiographical trace clearly organises the raw biographical data here – Stevenson's improved health, London's alarming illnesses – it does so to foreground an outlook in contradiction to this experiential actuality. There is clearly some other relationship determining the contradictory tone of these respective passages. From Stevenson's we would expect some of the 'jubilation' that travelling and improved health clearly brought him. For London, we would expect an anticipation of the agonising failure of the voyage; a recognition of the limitations of the human will. To recall Murphy's comment, there is clearly an 'active relationship of mutual contradiction' between experiential reality and its metaphorical ordering through autobiographical writing (Murphy 1972: 121).

To understand this contradiction we must understand the broader dialectical relationships that are focused in these texts. So far, in relation to the metaphorical utilisation of illness, we have identified the experiential (actual illness) and its figurative role in autobiographical representation. However, we must also consider external representation (physical effects) and internal (psychological) response. This can only be achieved by an analysis of cultural preconception itself both an internalisation of ideology and its external discursive constraints. This is most in evidence here through metaphors of illness, colonialism, and racial hierarchies. The use of the terms 'external' and 'internal' here is not intended to encourage a static binaristic thought. Internal response is articulated externally and is hence in a dialectical relationship with both the experiential (travel and illness) and its metaphorical ordering (writing).

It is also in a dialectical relationship with cultural preconception. This process is complex and extremely rich in signification – both authorially intended and otherwise – in contrast to the reductionism of Sontag and Derrida. As we have already seen for the former metaphor obscures truth and for the latter experience excludes writing (seen as a metaphorical ordering of self-presence). My argument is that this either/or approach travesties the dialectical richness by which self, culture and experience are mediated.

So, with Stevenson's and London's representation of illness and travel we might begin by considering the implications of this internal and external facet of the dialectical process. I suggested above that 'internal' related to the psychological with all this suggests of inner processes. However, I am here concerned with materiality, rather than some speculative attempt to psychoanalyse either of these two authors. We can only rely on what is betrayed by the autobiographical trace in relationship to the experiential (illness) by returning to the two primary passages from *In the South Seas* and *The Cruise of the Snark*. Whilst Stevenson characterises his frame of mind at the beginning of his voyage as an epilogue to his life and the prelude to another journey, towards death, it is also to be carried 'among scenes that had attracted me in youth and health' (3). So a journey into the unknown is also an imaginative/projected return to the familiar territory of youth and a recapturing of health. Reaching the known through the unknown, as it were. Moreover, a childish/adolescent orientation towards the whole affair. One might recall the high excitement that Lloyd Osbourne's use of 'jubilation' evokes. Indeed, the mention of nursing, immobility and being carried around suggests an involuntary infantilisation.

The despair of serious illness seems to authorise both maudlin self-dramatisation as an invalid resigned to death, contrasted with an incessant restlessness which, in turn, leads to an escapist infantilism. Read against Stevenson's real illness, its apparent remission in the South Pacific together with both his idealisation and robust introduction to the real brutalities of colonialism he encountered almost every day, the effect again seems to be one of contradiction. Stevenson seldom refers directly to his own poor health, but seems fascinated by the variety of illnesses suffered by the Polynesians, their population decline following European contact and colonialism, and particularly attitudes towards death. In the following passage, one can see all these themes at work together with a backward reference to an overpopulated Britain which, he implies, incubates disease:

> When I had sat down with them on the floor, the girl began to question me about England; which I tried to describe . . . explaining as best as I was able, and by word and gesture, the over-population, the hunger, and the perpetual toil. '*Pas de cocotiers? Pas de popoi?*' she asked. I told her it was too cold. But she understood right well; remarked it must be bad for the health, and sat a while gravely reflecting on that picture of unwonted sorrows . . . she began with a smiling sadness, and looking on me out of melancholy eyes, to lament the decrease of her own people. '*Ici pas de Kanaques*,' said she; and taking the baby from her breast, she held it out to me with both her hands. '*Tenez*' – a little baby like this; then dead. All the Kanaques die. Then no more. (Stevenson 1924, 23–4)

The following chapter (Chapter IV) is emphatically headed 'Death' and concerns itself with a detailed list of imported diseases and the dramatic population decline amongst the Marquesans.

Yet this passage also recreates the pessimistic atmosphere with

which Stevenson opens the book, emphasised by his representation of
the Marquesan woman's manner of speaking, variously characterised as
'gravely reflecting', 'smiling sadness', 'unwonted sorrows', and 'melancholy eyes'. Here Stevenson meets face to face with 'declining health',
'the afterpiece of life', a ghostly image of an earlier vital self projected,
perhaps displaced, onto an entire people. But note how Stevenson
arranges this scene: they all sit on the mat, prior to the woman's
despairing summation he enacts a kind of mime 'piling the pan and
cocoa shells one upon another to represent the houses . . . I went
through an elaborate performance, shutting out draughts and crouching
over an imaginary fire' (Ibid.: 23). And all the while 'the unconscious
babe struggled to reach a pot of raspberry jam' (Ibid.: 24). They are all
playing on the floor; the aspect is one of an adult playing with his child.
By the close of the chapter, the reader becomes aware of an oddly
jarring note:

> . . . and in a perspective of centuries I saw their case as ours, death
> coming in like a tide, and the day already numbered when there
> should be no more Beretani [Britain] and no more of any race
> whatever, and (what oddly touched me) no more literary works and
> no more readers. (24)

Not only is the slow, relentless, painful decline of illness displaced
but also the sense of infantilism. The tragic stature of the Marquesan
woman is undermined by her status as a quasi-child playing on the mat.
Not for her the the a return to happier times 'among scenes that had
attracted me in youth and health' (3). In fact, she and her island are
the scene of youthful attraction. Her case, and that of her people, is
terminal. But what of Stevenson and the European interloper that he
embodies? In very non-specific few centuries might they face a compar-
able situation. This represents a contradictory inversion of the child/
adult positions by which he, the European, at once claims youthful
vitality for his race but also the wisdom of age for it is he who goes
through an 'elaborate performance' for her enlightenment. He is both
the child *and* teacher. The child Marquesan suffers from the ignorance
of youth and the debilitation of old age which must, the logic implies,
give way to a younger generation – the European, or the white man.
    The passage betrays a keen sympathy over the common ground of
illness which pierces the ideological veil of colonialism; Stevenson
leaves us in no doubt that Europeans are to blame for the destructive
epidemics among the Marquesans. Crucially, the cause is the poor

climate of England and the transplantation of its diseases to the Marqueasas, much as Stevenson is himself so transplanted. But the discursive focalisation of colonialism reasserts itself even here: the Marquesans are a colonised people – 'natives' – whose power of comprehension and feeling must be childlike. The dialectic here is strained but revealing. The experience of individual and racial suffering is fractured into three autobiographical metaphors. The first, one of sympathy: pain is a shared experience. Secondly, an anti-colonial aversion to the ravages brought on by European contact. Thirdly, the reassertion of internalised imperial ideology: the mature, enlightened European infantilises the supplicant child-native. Stevenson depicts his own ill health as an infantilisation which is, in turn, displaced onto the Marquesans suffering under the effects of European engendered epidemic.

Another undercurrent to this passage is that Stevenson is not the first literary visitor to this part of the Marquesas, for this is the setting for Herman Melville's *Typee*. So when he writes of his own literary extinction – 'no more literary works and no more readers' – it is in the full knowledge that he is a participant in a literary history, a tradition. What is striking here, is that tradition seems to authorise an imaginary self- and racial-extinction with no risk to the reflective subject. In contrast, the Marquesans face an emphatically real termination of disease and depopulation. To return once again to his introductory passage, we can compare this with the anticipation of his own death that we find there. The 'afterpiece of life' is not only the real threat of death, but also imaginative play. For Stevenson, the reality of ending – death – through illness engenders literary beginnings: a figurative rebirth.

Parallel to this real and metaphorical search for better health, we find its externalised negative realisation in the plight of the Marquesans. What we find here is a devastating metaphorical mapping of Western Imperialism hidden below the rather jaunty style of the literary traveller. Figuratively, he is filling in a little more of the blank page of the romanticised metaphorical Marquesas first opened up by Melville. But more than this, the overpopulation of Britain and its incubation of disease fuels colonial expansion in a collective search for its own revitalisation in the contrived empty spaces and healthy climes of the South Pacific. Both the literal and figurative occupation of the Marquesas leads to the destruction of the indigenous population onto whom – literally and metaphorically – disease and atrophy are displaced. The effect is as disturbing as anything Conrad found in the Congo.

Stevenson, I would argue, is only partly conscious of what he reveals here. As we have already noted, on a conscious level he was certainly sympathetic to the Marquesans' fate, recognising both on an individual and broader basis that colonialism was to blame. He was no imperial apologist, as his political entanglements on behalf of the Samoans against the colonial government demonstrates. Equally, for a child of his time, he was relatively free of racism (Furnas 1951: 275). Yet we can clearly see how the internalisation of an ideology of travel to and occupation of another place provides the metaphorical ordering of his experiences and memories that is autobiography. That process simultaneously interacts with imperial ideology on an unconscious level, even as it is both materially and discursively resisted. Thence we find the Marquesans infantilised and cast as the passive receptor for the horror of diseases bred in the crowded cities and supposedly infelicitous climate of Europe. Colonial expansion is not only the displacement of peoples, but of cultural neuroses. The effect recalls Pierre Macherey's observation: 'the speech of the book comes from a certain silence, a matter which it endows with form, a ground on which it traces a figure. Thus, the book is not self-sufficient; it is necessarily accompanied by a *certain absence*, without which it would not exist' (Macherey 1990: 217).[5] Replace book with autobiography, and experience and memory become the matter on which a figure is traced. The silence is an internalised imperial ideology that figuratively struggles in a dialectical relationship with conscious intent to order the whole. What results is structural contradiction.

By December 1907, when Jack London, Charmian and their crew made landfall on the Marquesas he was consciously following in the wake of both Melville and Stevenson. We have already noted how London's introductory paragraph presents almost the opposite tone to Stevenson's, as does the progression of their illnesses. For London: from health to sickness, from an exaltation of the power of human will to despairing helplessness of defeat. Yet like Stevenson, London was also struck by the Marquesans diseased misery and depopulation, the point of departure again being Melville's *Typee*:

> Life faints and stumbles and gasps itself away. In this warm, equable clime – a truely terrestrial paradise – where are never extremes of temperature and where the air is like a balm, kept ever pure by the ozone-laden Southeast trade, asthma, pthisis, and tuberculosis flourish as luxuriantly as the vegetation. Everywhere, from the few

[5] The emphasis is Macherey's.

grass huts, arises the racking cough or exhausted groan of wasted lungs. Other horrible diseases prosper as well, but the most deadly of all are those that attack the lungs. There is a form of consumption called 'galloping,' which is especially dreaded. In two months time it reduces the strongest man to a skeleton under a grave-cloth. In valley after valley the last inhabitant has passed and the fertile soil has relapsed to jungle. (163)

The individual Marquesan is entirely absent from this scene. Rather than the melancholy of slow extinction which characterised Stevenson's passage, conferring a certain dignity on the surface (even if undermined by the child-like rendering), the Marquesans are practically invisible. Indeed, they are entirely displaced by the diseases that are consuming them. And yet the passage hesitates between implying that the Marquesans have succumbed to a congenital weakness – since the climate is so fine, it must be the people rather than the disease – that it is the disease itself that has flourished in this 'equable clime' and 'terrestrial paradise'. The contradiction is repeated in relation to the racial identity of the Marquesans. 'A pure Marquesan is a rare thing' writes London, 'They seem to be all half breeds and strange conglomerations of dozens of different races' (163). Initially, London ascribes what remaining vitality these people have to this hybridisation, 'the one thing that retards their destruction is the infusion of fresh blood' but later switches to contempt: 'it is a wreckage of races at best' (Ibid.).

What is clear is that ostensibly London refuses to directly countenance the possibility that the Marquesans' diseased condition and decline is the direct consequence of Western intervention. The blame either lies with the climate (the very thing, we might recall, Stevenson says of England) or the extreme hybridisation which causes the modern Marquesan's lack of initiative and energy. He concludes this descriptive passage with the observation that, through lack of cultivation, the land reverts to a jungle condition which no doubt leaves it free to be recovered by Europeans. The people have been defeated by the land and their fall from racial purity either hastens or retards that defeat. Lying beneath London's contempt is a horror of both impurity and the ability of nature to lay humanity low. It is a lack of will that leads to decline, which sits uncomfortably with the thwarting of London's own will when the voyage is abandoned due to his own tropical sicknesses.

Yet such fear might stem from more unconscious anxieties. London's own 'race' occupies usurped land and, by the early twentieth century the people of the United States had become a by-word as a cultural and racial melting-pot. Ironically, many of the peoples he detects in the admixture of Marquesansan blood, are akin to those found in the modern 'white' American: 'English, American, Dane, German, French, Corsican, Spanish, Portuguese, Chinese . . .' (163). A small part of London's own family history is emblematic of such 'hybridisation', being the son of another man than his mother's husband. His natural father denied paternity. Not surprisingly, London returns later in the chapter to this theme in an attempt to exorcise both the contradictions of his position on racial purity/hybridisation and his claims to 'racial superiority'. Once again the focus is on illness. Now he is more emphatic, the Marquesans described by Melville were 'physically magnificent [because racially] they were pure' (163). To deal with his own nations' famed 'hybridity', London refers broadly to the purity of the 'white race' and now acknowledges that white men brought disease to the Marquesas. Because the 'white race' is relatively more diseased and has developed resistance, it is of greater vigour because its purity is refined by natural selection:

> We of the white race are the survivors and the descendants of the thousands of generations of survivors in the war with micro-organisms. Whenever one of us is born with a constitution peculiarly receptive to these minute enemies, such a one promptly died. Only these of us survived who could withstand them. We who are alive are the immune, the fit – the ones best constituted to live in a world of hostile micro-organisms. The poor Marquesans had undergone no such selection. They were not immune. (London 1971: 170)

London even manages to make a cannibal joke of it: because the Marquesans ate their enemies, they ingested 'white' diseases all the quicker. That this is an ideologically motivated application of Darwin's theory is hardly a matter of debate. But considered as a whole, London's response to the plight of the Marquesans is marked by contradiction at every turn. Hybridity destroys purity but confers energy; pure Marquesans were physically magnificent, but inherently weak; it is the place and climate which encourages disease, or rather the climate and place has nothing to do with it; white people carry innumerable diseases which wipe out a people, but are physically immune themselves. Yet London enjoys no immunity from Pacific diseases and hardly comes from a 'pure' race in his sense of the term.

His final word on the matter brings us to a similar position to that of Stevenson. If, he suggests, the Marquesans had been a people of several hundred thousands rather than a few thousands they might have survived the bacteriological onslaught. They may even have been strengthened. The implication suppressed within the text is that it is European overpopulation and expansion that has created this con-tinual expansion Westwards. Overpopulation perhaps accounts for its relatively diseased history. With no colonial expansion there would have been no contact and the Marquesans would have continued to enjoy a vigorous life. It is colonialism itself which again interacts both with conscious ideological attempt to transfer guilt and personal anxieties fixated around disease, both real and figurative. According to London, the invasion of Europeans is akin to a plague of disease carrying creatures from the Marqueasan perspective. Again, colonial expansion is not only the displacement of peoples, but cultural neuroses.

The conclusion to be drawn from London's contradictions is that the organisation of memory and experiences through metaphor cuts many ways. A representative of an unquestionably effective Western imperi-alism, he figuratively casts himself as an empowered overman; hence the emphasis on strength of will triumphing over nature. Yet the dialectic here exposes the consequences of that power. As the white man he is akin to a Darwinian angel of death carrying disease over the world; power of a sort perhaps, but of questionable distinction. In fact London attempts to recast the destruction and misery wrought by European expansion and colonialism as a positive force. Any blame must be displaced onto nature – 'natural selection'. But this leaves him personally disempowered for he is just as susceptible to new diseases as the Marquesan he lords over. The twist and turns of London's writing as he attempts to escape the implications of these contradictions demonstrates the impossibility of containing metaphors such as illness which draw on a multi-faceted dialectic, here mediating between experiential reality, autobiographical metaphor, colonial ideology and various cultural discourses. As Rousseau wrote: 'Perhaps his system is false; but in developing it, he has painted himself truly.'

For both Stevenson and London, personal experience of illness and its derived metaphors creates a dialectic which forms an uneasy passage between internalised fears and anxieties; an externalised sympathy for the suffering of others; and colonial and racial ideologies. The nature of the autobiographical trace is such that conscious attempts to organise experience cannot exclude those unwanted, obscured facets of the dialectical process. Metaphor, anchored in this instance on illness, mediates between experience and the imagination which is shaped, in turn, by the author's own will and personality and also cultural discourse of which racial and imperial ideologies of colonialism are dominant here. The consequence, as Simmel observes, is:

> . . . the deep estrangement or animosity which exists between the organic and creative products of the soul and its contents and products: the vibrating, restless life of the creative soul, which develops toward the infinite contrasts with its fixed and ideally changing product and its uncanny feedback effect, which arrests and indeed rigidifies this liveliness. Frequently it appears as if the creative movement of the soul were dying of its own product. (Simmel 1968: 31)

Both Stevenson's and London's responses to illness in the Marquesas and their self-presentation through autobiography, reveal two 'acceptable' faces of nineteenth-century colonialism. The condescending paternalism of Stevenson which creates the child-native, matched by London's celebration of the 'superiority' of the white race as the chosen of nature. Whatever their suppressed contradictions, these are the essential characterisations that emerge from the passages we have examined. Yet, through their focus on illness and their personal sufferings, a third aspect of colonialism emerges: one far from authorised, or positive. It is of the colonist, the European, as both parasite and carrier of pestilence. This aspect is the cry of the oppressed which cannot be excluded since it belongs to the same dialectical continuum. A metaphor, of course, but an involuntary betrayal of a bad conscience nonetheless.

Works Cited

Barltrop, Robert, 1976. *Jack London: The Man, the Writer, the Rebel*, London: The Pluto Press.

Edmond, Rod, 1997. 'Leprosy and Colonial Discourse: Jack London and Hawaii', *Wasafiri* 25 (Spring), 78–82.

——, 1997. *Representing the South Pacific: Colonial Discourse from Cook to Gauguin*, Cambridge: Cambridge University Press.

Frye, Northrop, 1991. 'The Expanding World of Metaphor', in *Northrop Frye: Myth and Metaphor: Selected Essays 1974–1988*, ed. Robert D. Denham, Charlottesville and London: University Press of Virginia, 108–23.

Furnas, J.C., 1950. *Anatomy of Paradise: Hawaii and the Islands of the South Seas*, London: Gollancz.

——, 1951. *Voyage to Windward: The Life of Robert Louis Stevenson*, New York: William Slaone.

Kirby, Kathleen M., 1996. *Indifferent Boundaries: Spatial Concepts of Human Subjectivity*, New York and London: The Guildford Press.

Knight, Alanna (ed.), 1986. *R. L. S. In the South Seas: An Intimate Photographic Record*, Edinburgh: Mainstream Publishing.

London, Charmian Kittredge, n.d. *A Woman Among the Headhunters: A Narrative of the Voyage of the 'Snark' in the Years 1908–1909*, London: Mills & Boon.

London, Jack, 1971. *The Cruise of the Snark*, London: Seafarer Books.

London, Joan, 1968. *Jack London and his Times: An Unconventional Biography*, Seattle and London: University of Washington Press.

Macherey, Pierre, 1990. 'The Text Says What it Does Not Say', trans. G. Wall in *Literature in the Modern World: Critcal Essays and Documents*, ed. Dennis Walder, Oxford: Oxford University Press, 215–22.

Maude, H.E., 1968. *Of Islands and Men: Studies in Pacific History*, Melbourne: Oxford University Press.

McLynn, Frank, 1993. *Robert Louis Stevenson: A Biography*, London: Hutchinson.

Melville, Herman, 1950. *Typee: A Real Romance of the South Seas*, Boston: L.C. Page & Co.

——, 1969. *Omoo: A Narrative of Adventures in the South Seas*, New York: Hendricks House.

Murphy, Robert F., 1972. *The Dialectics of Social Life: Alarms and Excursions in Anthropological Theory*, London: George Allen & Unwin.

Oliver, Douglas L., 1962. *The Pacific Islands*, Cambridge, Mass: Harvard University Press.

Olney, 1972. *Metaphors of Self: The Meaning of Autobiography*, Princeton: Princeton University Press.

Paterson, Bill, 1984. *Rifled Sanctuaries: Some Views of the Pacific Islands in Western Literature to 1900*, Auckland: Auckland University Press and Oxford University Press.

Ralston, Caroline, 1977. *Grass Huts and Warehouses: Pacific Beach Communities of the Nineteenth Century*, Canberra: Australian National University Press.

Rennies, Neil, 1995. *Far-Fetched Facts: The Literature of Travel and the Idea of the South Seas*, Oxford: Clarendon Press.

Silverman, Hugh J., 1994. *Textualities: Between Hermeneutics and Deconstruction*, New York and London: Routledge.

Sontag, Susan, 1983. *Illness as Metaphor*, Harmondsworth: Penguin.

Stanley, Liz, 1992. *The Auto/Biographical I: The Theory and Practice of Feminist Auto/Biography*, Manchester and New York: Manchester University Press.

Stevenson, Robert Louis, 1924. *In the South Seas*, London: William Heinemann.

——, 1926. *Vailima Letters: Being Correspondence from R.L. Stevenson to Sidney Colvin, November 1890 – October 1894*, London: Methuen.

Stevenson, R.L., and Fanny Stevenson, 1956. *Our Samoan Adventure*, London: Weidenfeld and Nicolson.

Pop Goes the Centre:
Hanif Kureishi's London

SUKHDEV SANDHU

FROM THE SLAVE AUTOBIOGRAPHY Ukawsaw Gronniosaw produced in 1772 to the rash of hardboiled, scumsurfing thrillers scribbled in recent years by Victor Headley, Donald Gorgon and Q, nearly all those swarthy writers hailing from the English empire who've put pen to paper in this country have written about London. Regardless of which continent they hail from, their age, gender, or sexual preference, they've all described the capital directly and indirectly, at greater or lesser length, and in a variety of genres – travel memoirs, fiction, poetry, polemical essays, radio drama and, in the case of Fred D'Aguiar's *Sweet Thames* (1992), television poem. Such tawny metrography has gone largely unnoticed. A.N. Wilson's *Faber Book of London* (1994) excerpted Lord Scarman's report into the Brixton Riots of 1981, but didn't include any passages from books by Asian, African or Caribbean writers themselves.

The upsurge in black British historiography over the last couple of decades has failed to inspire literary scholars to braid together different periods and writers to see if certain themes and tropes keep recurring down the centuries. Given the recent 'geographic turn' in literary and critical theory, it's particularly surprising that no one has seized on the importance of London to black authors. Cartographies of desire, landscapes of memory, mappings of power – one would expect this geographic register to trigger an interest in the historical and social materiality that poststructuralism has shirked. Unfortunately, spatial rhetoric is often used loosely and metaphorically. Postcolonial criticism bandies about concepts such as 'centre', 'margin' and 'metropolis' with decontextualized and hectoring abandon. And to assume without nuance, without subtle and historical inflection – as so much theory does – that the colonial individual's relationship to the capital is one of peripheral genuflection to a swaggering and condescending imperial centre is plain tiresome.

This is made luminously clear by the work of the Anglo-Pakistani novelist, dramatist and film-maker Hanif Kureishi. Academics and – more importantly – fellow artists have cited him as the canniest and most entertaining chronicler of the black British experience. London, both its allure and abjection, has been the dominant theme of his writings ever since the publication of *Borderline* in 1981. This essay – subdivided into sections on suburbia, Home, messiness and velocity, collage, sex – explores Kureishi's fascination with the capital and spells out what distinguishes his writing about London from that of black and Asian authors before him.

Kureishi (b.1954) is London's first major cartographer of Asian or Caribbean descent to have been born in England itself. He was brought up in Bromley, Kent, a borough 10 miles south of London Bridge, and a 20 minute train journey from Victoria. Long seen as quintessentially suburban, Bromley is neither truly urban nor rural but, in the eyes of its critics, marooned somewhere in-between, a lingering and painful half-life. Architects and cultural commentators often claim suburbia represents a flight from the inner city's vitality. It's also been held responsible for generating traffic jams, for being a monotonous sprawl, and for symbolizing the triumph of individual expression over communality.

Kureishi's objections aren't so much aesthetic or architectural as social and ethical. In *The Buddha of Suburbia* (1990), Karim, the novel's ambitious (and deeply autobiographical) narrator, slags off the dull materialism of suburbia: the people of Chislehurst 'would exchange their legs for: velvet curtains, stereos, Martinis, electric lawnmowers' (51). Indeed, 'it was said that when people drowned they saw not their lives but their double-glazing flashing before them' (23).

Kureishi believes that suburban residents don't care for education in anything other than an instrumental sense. They decry forms of culture that challenge or disrupt their self-identities, that seek to extend – rather than merely confirm – established modes of thought or structures of feeling. In *The Black Album* (1995), Shahid leaves Sevenoaks because the people there aren't interested in culture, 'but only gardening guides, atlases, Reader's Digests' (22). In *Buddha*, Karim envies those who can 'talk of art, theatre, architecture, travel; the languages, the vocabulary, knowing the way round a whole culture – it was invaluable and irreplaceable capital' (177). Such capital abounds, as it were, in the capital.

Kureishi thinks that suburbia is incorrigibly xenophobic. The adolescent and idealistic Asians he creates – Haroon, Karim and Shahid – must move away or, inevitably, be fucked over. This is no casually obscene metaphor. Karim, in *Buddha*, goes to visit his girlfriend Helen, but is repelled by her father who proudly announces, ' "We're with Enoch" ' (40). Karim turns to leave but, before he can do so, is trapped against the garden fence by the family's Great Dane who clambers amorously over him and bestows him generously with trails of deepest jissom. What a fate! What an epiphany! Buggered by a (racist) Englishman's best friend, his dog, in those suburbs which, according to Eva in *Birds of Passage* ('if you want to see what England's really like, come out to Chislehurst sometime'), embody all that's best about this country (in *Outskirts*, 181). Karim flees to London with all the desperation and relief of the political refugee.

It's not only such treatment from white people (and their dogs) that makes Kureishi's characters want to move away. Pressure is also imposed from within the Asian community. In *Borderline*, which is set in Ealing, an area with a high concentration of Asians, Haroon complains to his girlfriend Amina, 'All of us. Shut in for safety. Strong and solid now. But stifled here together. Here my brain feels like a tight ball' (in *Outskirts*, 117). It's this sense of constriction and being hemmed-in which makes London's fluidity and looseness so joyous.

Kureishi has written at length about how important pop music was to him as he grew up and how its pulsation, speed and sensuality influenced his ideas about the subjects literature should cover as well as the effect it should have on its readers. From Dion's 'The Wanderer' (1962), to Steppenwolf's 'Born to be Wild' (1969), right through to Springsteen's 'Born to Run' (1975) and even Oasis' 'Live Forever' (1994), the urge to be free, mobile, and to escape from the shackles of domesticity have been central motifs of all pop. Many of the groups who were most successful as Kureishi was growing up scorned suburbia as that deadening zone where, as the Bonzo Dog Doo-Dah Band sniggered, 'My pink side of the drainpipe keeps me away from you'.

Lower middle-class boys like Mick Jagger, Ray Davies and David Bowie felt that questions of race, sexuality and self-identity could all be explored more easily and creatively if they moved to London. It was there that Lennon and McCartney went to parties hosted by Harold Pinter, met Bertrand Russell, became entranced by Indian transcendentalism after attending lectures by the Maharishi Mahesh Yogi, exchanged shorn hair with the murderous black radical Michael X, in return for a bloodied pair of Muhammad Ali's boxing shorts, and dined and fraternized with pop artists such as Peter Blake and Richard Hamilton.

David Bowie, or David Jones as he was then known, moved from

Brixton to Plaistow Grove in Bromley at an early age. He attended the same school as Karim where 'Boys were often to be found on their knees before this icon, praying to be made into pop stars and for release from a lifetime as a motor-mechanic' (68). And it was Bowie whose escape from suburbia and 'from class, from sex, from personality, from obvious commitment' into London's wide realm of free play, make-believe and self-gratification, is a trajectory that comes closest to the odysseys undertaken by Kureishi's characters (Thomson, xxii). It's for freedom that Shahid comes to London, so he's particularly annoyed when his relatives try to drag 'him back into an earlier self and life, one he had gratefully sloughed off' (158).

Suburbia's only function, then, is to serve as 'a leaving place' (*Outskirts*, 173; *Buddha*, 117). The cruellest insult Nina can hurl at Nadia as the latter steps off a plane in 'With Your Tongue Down My Throat' is 'you look as if you live in Enfield' (in *Love in a Blue Time*, 67).

More than just suburbia itself though, it's the sanctification of home which precludes Kureishi's characters from truly living, and which stymies their attempts to enjoy the heterotopian possibilities of metropolitan life.

'WELCOME HOME' proclaimed the *Evening Standard* the day before the *SS Empire Windrush* docked at Tilbury on 22 June 1948. It was a generous and, unwittingly, historically freighted headline to greet the first shipload of post-war immigrants to England. From Ignatius Sancho to Caryl Phillips, accounts of London by writers of Asian and African descent have been obsessed with the idea of home. To raise the money to buy a house in the capital, to have the means to maintain one's family, to have somewhere in the cold metropolis that one could unequivocally call one's own – these have been the central objectives of authors as disparate as Gronniosaw and Selvon. 'There is no such word as "home" in our language', wrote the Nawab Mehdi Hasan Khan in 1890, 'I had heard the word so often that I was anxious to see an English house and real home life' (Hobhouse, 62). His fixation is understandable. A home provides stability and reassurance. It's a mark of social progress. Owning one means that there's no longer the regular panic about monthly rent payments, of being kicked out of the premises by curmudgeonly Westbourne Grove landlords, or having to trudge dispiritedly from hostel to hostel for new accommodation. Above all, a home of one's own is a mark of great respectability.

Kureishi's characters, however, grew up with such domestic comforts and securities. They took them for granted and now seek less settled, less orderly worlds. The more hackneyed trappings of domesticity and the familial realm are only prized by Kureishi's less appealing fictional creations. In *London Kills Me* (1991), Lily, wife of the gun-toting, Elvis-obsessed pornographer, Stone, is embarrassingly proud of how her house, one without books, has been 'done up'.

During the course of *Buddha*, Eva becomes a successful interior designer. One could view this job positively: it symbolizes our desire and our need to refashion and transform ourselves. On the other hand, it's a job which panders to the belief that a new wall-unit or colour combination amounts to a meaningful improvement in the quality of one's life. Interior designers are actually obsessed with the exteriority of human lives – the cosmetic as opposed to the ethical.

Buddha, which ends on the night of the 1979 General Election, maps in advance the new contours that Conservatism would so successfully assume in the 1980s. By portraying Eva as a designer, Kureishi is able to isolate one of the key arenas in which the battle between Left and Right was fought during that decade – the housing market.

London saw a much-heralded rise in luxury developments. Gentrification led to moneyed professionals moving into previously unfashionable areas such as Clapham and Notting Hill. Working class people were told that the right to buy their council houses was a substantive step towards empowerment and social enfranchisement. There was a housing boom: at one point in 1985, the value of a three bedroomed suburban cottage in Beckenham could be expected to appreciate by a thousand pounds a week.

But there was also a darker side to the capital's housing market. Analysts have highlighted the under-investment in new buildings and pointed to the decline in private rented accommodation which led to a huge rise in the number of people sleeping rough under the Embankment, in the doorways of Covent Garden restaurants, and huddled amidst the dustbins and detrita behind Irish pubs in Camden.

Kureishi was repelled by these changes. In 'Finishing The Job', a 1988 essay on that year's Conservative Party Conference, he writes with palpable distaste that

> Walking past the houses of my childhood I noticed how, in an orgy of alteration they had been 'done up' . . . It was DIY they loved in Thatcherland, not self-improvement or culture or food, but prosperity, bigger and better homes complete with every mod-con – the concrete display of hard-earned cash. Display was the game. (19)

Such a concern for DIY can lead to the prioritization of buildings, and their potential profitability, at the expense of a concern for the well-being of their inhabitants. Eviction, the inevitable outcome of this mentality, features in *Borderline*, *Laundrette* and *London Kills Me*. Kureishi's hatred of suburbia and home come together in *Sammy* when Rosie reveals that her 'crude, vicious, racist and ignorant' father was not only the Mayor of Bromley, but – shame! – ran a furniture store.

So it's clear that Conservative ideology in the 1980s supplies a crucial context for Kureishi's repeated depictions of metropolitan housing. The right to buy, to 'do up' one's house with furniture bought from Habitat and Ikea became an extension of the traditional Tory belief in the sacred importance of property. This view draws on the idea of an Englishman's home being his castle. Such a metaphor, with its implicit suggestion of the house as a fortress and defence against intruders, was concretized and racialized in *The Buddha of Suburbia*'s 'dog-fuck' scene.

Houses are also of huge symbolic importance to first generation Asian immigrants. Since the 1960s they've achieved high owner occupier rates. They also have the most inhabitants per household of any ethnic group. Male settlers had to save enough money to bring over their dependants and this made them reluctant to go out socializing. This tendency continued after the arrival of their spouses and, combined with religious codes which restricted the freedom of their children – especially that of their daughters – meant that the domestic sphere took on a highly privileged place within Asian cultural life. If many Asian parents were beset by a limited grasp of the English language, and shied away through suspicion and timidity from the exigencies of social life, then, at least, they knew that upon returning home they were entering a controlled, less complicated zone where they could impress upon their children the religious, matrimonial and educational imperatives that they themselves held so dear.

None of Kureishi's more lovable or deserving creations lives in a wholly tidy, respectable or 'hygienic' house. In *Laundrette*, Omar's alcoholic father, who'd been a famous and radical journalist back in Pakistan, has a 'small, damp and dirty' flat in South London which 'hasn't been decorated for years' (51). Omar's boyfriend, Johnny, used to be a squatter before he moved into a noisy, rundown house full of arrogant Pakistani students. In *Buddha*, Jamila leaves her family home to enter a commune full of rotting tarpaulins and leaking pipes, one which is inhabited by radical lawyers, vegetarians, intellectual lesbians and jazz-lovers. Here, ties of blood matter less than collective goodwill and mutual commitment. In *London Kills Me*, Clint's posse occupy a flat in Whitehall Gardens which, for all its problems, seems far more pleasureable and vital than his mum's fraught, niggly set-up with Stone.

Similarly, almost none of the people who live in more conventional or lucrative properties are shown in a positive or enviable light. In *Buddha*, Karim takes part in an orgy in the four-storeyed, Indian-friezed, and highly tasteful St. John's Wood mansion of the theatre director Matthew Pyke, who is, notwithstanding, repulsively bloodless and manipulative. Karim's girlfriend, Eleanor, has a lovely Notting Hill pad, a wealthy family, important and powerful connections, but she's still emotionally scarred by the suicide of her black boyfriend, Gene. In *London Kills Me*, the college professor, Headley, despite her arty and tasteful flat, is cold and self-obsessed.

Kureishi rejects the idea that having a stable, well decked-out house is an important signifier of either a person's moral worth or their social likability. Bricks and mortar, and the rootedness they help to supply, can't guarantee universal and unconditional happiness. By depicting – with sympathy and approval – crumbling households, unorthodox communities and designs for living that are piecemeal, contingent and slung-together, Kureishi reveals a vision of the metropolis that's as radical as it is inimical to both Thatcherite and traditional Asian notions of domestic and social propriety.

This interest in the brokenness, the unrespectable and the more chaotic aspects of London recurs throughout Kureishi's work. In *Buddha*, Karim recalls the train journeys from Bromley he used to take as a youth with his Uncle Ted, in order to watch Chelsea play at Stamford Bridge: 'Before crossing the river we passed over the slums of Herne Hill and Brixton, places so compelling and unlike anything I was used to seeing that I jumped up, jammed down the window and gazed out at the rows of disintegrating Victorian houses. The gardens were full of rusting junk and sodden overcoats; lines of washing criss-crossed over the debris' (43). The sensation of speed, the novelty of these environments, and the fact that these are lawnmower-free zones all magnetize the adolescent Karim.

Even when Kureishi's characters do arrive in the capital, this readiness to find value in localities and lifestyles that others would regard as unpleasant persists. The directions to *My Beautiful Laundrette* order Omar to walk '*along a South London street, towards NASSER'S garage. It's a rough area, beautiful in its own falling-down way*' (53).

Passages like these display a manifest commitment to the culture and vitality of the inner city, no matter how rundown or neglected it may have become, that's deeply political. Following the abolition of the Greater London Council in 1986, the capital lacked its own democratically elected governing body for the first time since the establishment of the London City Corporation in 1888. No central planning or administrative body existed to tackle the growing problems of social polarization, unemployment, and an emerging underclass. It seemed to many, including the directors of such films as *Empire State* (1986) and *Close My Eyes* (1991), that rentiers, unelected city quangos and foreign capital had taken governance of the capital. At the close of *Sammy and Rosie Get Laid*, the ramshackle homes of the community that's been forged by the junkies, beggars and homeless people under a motorway bridge are bulldozed whilst a property developer announces proudly that he's 'making London a cleaner and safer place' (55).

Kureishi deems this a bogus form of hygiene. He feels that any attempt to deny the mess, the confusion and the contamination that's central to all urban life, is ideologically and intellectually dubious. There's a parallel between the property developer's attitude towards London and that of the Islamic fundamentalist, Riaz, in *The Black Album*. Early in this novel, Riaz is shown walking the streets 'rapidly in a straight line. To keep up, and to avoid charging into the Irishmen who gathered outside the pubs, Shahid had to jig on and off the pavement' (2). The property developer wants to clean up London in order to allow the swifter flow and accumulation of capital by multinational corporations. Riaz wants to clean up London – and Western society – by diverting people from the path of secularization and, instead, leading them to Allah. Both views, for Kureishi, tend to downgrade and emulsify the histories, lives and hopes of the millions of people who shuffle through the streets of London every day.

At some time or another, most of Kureishi's characters feel the need for change, to break out of the ruts that they find themselves in. Mobility, transformation, turnover – these are all qualities that cities allow for and encourage. Freed from family, from community, from the slower timeframes of suburban and provincial life, the city pell-mells with traffic, randomness, neon brightness and multiplicity. In *The Black Album*, Shahid and his tutor both share the same response to metropolitan life. Deedee enjoyed the feeling of 'speeding – towards what she had no idea. Nothing would hold her; velocity was all'. In *Sammy and Rosie Get Laid*, as Danny and Rafi walk down a tube tunnel, Kureishi writes in the directions that, 'As an expert, I suggest the tunnel that connects the Piccadilly with the Victoria Line at Green Park – a superb sensation you get here of endless walking in both directions' (18–19).

Kureishi's archetypal London landscape consists of young people abandoning their rooms and cruising through the streets of the capital, passing by myriads of multi-ethnic shops, restaurants and people; they'll smile, laugh, and imbibe both high and low culture. All of this will take place to the accompaniment of loud, pounding beats which capture young London's density, its ricocheting medley. In The Black Album Shahid and Deedee giggle their way through Islington; they kiss, wander past the shops selling Indian-print scarves or punk bootlegs, buy Greil Marcus and Flannery O'Connor books, visit pubs. 'It was rare to see anyone over forty, as if there were a curfew for older people' (93). This, for Shahid, is the life – the clamour, the culture, and the congestion that a suburban upbringing had left him gasping for. And it's with this aspect alone of London society – deregulated, energized, pop – that Kureishi's characters identify. They relate to the city not in terms of particular places – Selvon's Bayswater Road or Kwesi Johnson's Brixton street corners – but as a mood, an attitude of openness and brio. More than just a space, London represents an ideal – that of possibility, change, the transformation of both self and society. This ideal may be naive, absurdly utopian perhaps, but it's all the more 'pop' because of that. Sammy enthuses to his baffled father about the joys of kissing and arguing on Hammersmith towpath, strolling through Hyde Park, watching alternative comedians in Earl's Court abuse the Government and attending semiotic seminars at the ICA where Colin McCabe discusses 'The relation between a bag of crisps and the self-enclosed unity of the linguistic sign', before concluding 'We love our city and we belong to it. Neither of us are English, we're Londoners you see' (33).

It's an interesting remark and one which flies in the face of the doomy portraits of immigrant life in the metropolis normally painted by literary scholars and race relations experts. Though Kureishi's declaration of metrophilia is unusually explicit,[1] it joins a tradition of

---

[1] Though it's rivalled by one of Sam Selvon's short stories. '[W]hen she asked me why I loved London I too shrugged . . . The way St Paul's was, half-hidden in the rain, the motionless trees along the Embankment. But you say a thing like that and people don't understand at all. How sometimes a surge of greatness could sweep over you when you see something.' 'My Girl and the City', in Ways of Sunlight (London: MacGibbon and Kee, 1957).

positivity about London which ranges from Sancho's invocation of 'our grand metropolis' right throught to Lamming's affectionate accounts of cosmopolitan Hampstead, Rushdie's *The Satanic Verses* (1988) and *Junglist* (1995) by Two Fingers and James T. Kirk. These writers don't deny that life in the city can be jarring and turmoily, but they also feel that its diversity, ebullience and phatness more than compensate. Kureishi agrees; and although there's plenty of racial violence (Genghis' thuggish friends in *Laundrette*; the pigs heads hurled through the window of Anwar's South London grocery in *Buddha*; the daily attacks on Bengali estates in *The Black Album*), his work contains far more inter-racial mingling, fraternizing and couplings than that of previous writers. This is largely because Kureishi focusses on second generation Asians who are fascinated by and embroiled in pop culture, that realm at the 'fringes of the respectable world [where there is] marijuana, generational conflict, clubs, parties, and to a certain kind of guiltless, casual sex' (*Faber Book of Pop*, xix). English pop, unlike the American variety, has never been racially segregated or monochromatic. In fact, it's one of the few areas where class, race and background become subordinated to the eternal 'now' that is at the heart of pop music and where, as Rakim rapped, 'It ain't where you're from – it's where you're at' (Gilroy, 120). This dictum appeals to Kureishi's chief protagonists who, like Karim, don't always want to be defined by the values and beliefs of their parents.

Sammy's statement is also didactic and provocative rather than merely descriptive. It implicitly rejects the first generation Asian view that migration and geography make no difference, and that children should cleave to their parents. Nor does it simply endorse assimilationism, a line of thought which rarely acknowledges that the host society is itself composed of a welter of classes, regions and biographies. There's no simple, uniform Englishness with which anyone, yet alone an immigrant, could hope to assimilate. Sammy himself does not equate being a Londoner with being English.

A cant term in contemporary critical discourse is 'in-betweenness'. It involves a rejection of simplistic binarisms and oppositions such as colonizer/colonized, heterosexual/homosexual or margin/centre in favour of a more conjoined, 'hybridized' explanation of identity in which, as it were, forever the twain shall meet.

But Kureishi's relationship to the city differs from the three approaches outlined above. For him, it involves seeing London as a generator of *aggregation*, where he can wear as many masks, create as many personae, explore as many new avenues as he wishes. Not only does this view bypass the dualism implicit in the idea of hybridity, it also highlights the crucial importance of *place* in fomenting and facilitating such cross-cultural encounters. Kureishi's London throngs. It's multiplicitous. There's a freedom from homes, from families, from 'bourgeois' constraints which allows the likes of Omar, Karim and Shahid a limitless palette of intellectual, social and sexual combinations. Stepping out into West Kensington for the first time, Karim feels that 'being in a place so bright, fast and brilliant made you vertiginous with possibility' (126). It's this potential for self-fashioning and the constant mutation and updating of the self that terrifies fundamentalists like Riaz.

Similarly, in *The Buddha of Suburbia*, Karim becomes an actor, a job which involves the repeated donning and casting aside of costumes and personae. Attending the funeral of Anwar, his father's friend since boyhood, Karim begins to feel 'ashamed and incomplete' because he isn't sufficiently Indian (212). He makes a resolution: 'If I wanted the additional personality bonus of an Indian past, I would have to create it' (213). The key word here is 'create'. A sense of pastness may be fashioned from nothing, it's a 'personality bonus' – words that echo the rhetoric of a Liberty's sales campaign. History and tradition tend to become submerged in the rapid turnovers and upheavals of urban life.

Kureishi's London young people are always on the move. They cruise through the streets like Clint, up the social ladder like Karim, jump from one bed to another like the eponymous characters of *Sammy and Rosie Get Laid*. On the tube, at Islington parties and at art gallery private views, men and women of different races, classes, ages and nationalities bump into each other, gossip, fight, and try to pull. Such unexpected encounters are one of the defining features of metropolitan life: international financiers leaving expensive restaurants are touched for fivers by drink-sodden down and outs; impoverished students in Polish cafés are startled to see that the cabbage dishes they've ordered are being served by actors they'd grown up watching on daytime soaps; freshly uncloseted provincial boys stumble into the toilets of South London gay clubs only to witness Labour junior ministers being rimmed and fellated by a pair of 6' 4" Canadian musclemen called Erik and Barnes.

The likes of Karim and Shahid come to the capital precisely because they are entranced by its unpredictability and disorderliness. In *The Buddha of Suburbia*, Charlie argues that people should be appointed to jobs randomly: 'People in the street must be approached and told that they are now editor of *The Times* for a month' (88).

Juxtaposition and collage are the central techniques that Kureishi employs to create this collision-filled London. Collage was a favoured format of many English artists of the 1960s. For Gwyther Irwin and Stuart Brisley, 'The illicit, violent and socially transgressive was bound up in the process of image scavenging' (Mellor, 22). Peter Blake was the most famous deployer of collage and, with his then-wife, Jan Haworth, designed the cover of *Sgt. Pepper's Lonely Hearts Club Band* in 1967. Given Kureishi's love of The Beatles, it's perhaps unsurprising that he personally asked Blake to design the jacket for *The Buddha of Suburbia*.

Collage is a democratic art. Found images, tabloid pin-ups and pencil sketches can all be stitched together to produce original and arresting pieces. By juxtaposing figures of elevated social standing from high culture with pop icons and the urban underclass, collage creates a new imaginative space where no individual can insist on preserving a privileged zone or an unpolluted sphere from which members of other races and classes are barred. This merely reflects the quotidian exigencies of urban life: homeless Clint will find himself stealing food at private views or flirting with actresses at upmarket diners; Charlie will end up in nightclubs vomiting into the lap of a famous footballer; Eleanor, who's the daughter of a close friend of the Queen Mother, will mingle with Rasta dope dealers every time she goes to the pub, and will sleep with a 'grossly fat and ugly sixteen-stone' Scottish roadsweeper (*Buddha*, 175).

Juxtaposition, which lies at the heart of collage, often takes a linguistic form in Kureishi's work. In *My Beautful Laundrette*, Omar predicts great success for his business venture: 'It'll be going into profit any day now. Partly because I've hired a bloke of outstanding competence and strength of body and mind to look after it with me' (35).

These lines embody Kureishi's claim that 'Irony is the modern mode, a way of commenting on bleakness and cruelty without falling into dourness and didacticism' (*Laundrette*, 43). Omar's monetarist imperative and his vision of forthcoming financial bonanza is rendered both vacuous and horrid by his parroting of jargon which marries the rhetorics of corporate high finance and Hollywood biopic. The disjunction between the triumphalist language and its material basis (a measly launderette) is captured by the single word 'bloke' – the hyperbole rings hollow when all it's endorsing is this slangy monosyllable. There's a stilted quality to these lines which embodies the gulf between the rhetoric's dominant cultural and political sources and the working class origins of the rather gawky speaker.

Viewed in its entirety, *My Beautiful Laundrette* is a particularly good example of how juxtaposition can be didactic as well as descriptive. For, if cultural chauvinists believe that blackness and Britishness, or immigration and the nation's economic well-being are incompatible, Kureishi takes palpable delight in collapsing such polarities, in showing how London exists and thrives through the repeated jamming together of disparate groups. Here he juxtaposes a rundown vestige of a decayed past – a launderette called Churchill's – with two social lepers who decide to refashion it, and, in doing so, offer a startling example of how England may be saved from economic and cultural decline.

It's a highly significant act of transformation. Churchill is a symbol of an older England – he represents stability, the luxury of historical continuity, nostalgia and a certain strain of imperial aristocracy. His name was often invoked for nationalistic reasons by Margaret Thatcher during the Falklands War. He was also trusted by that older generation of Asian settlers who, in Kureishi's work, often check their children's drive towards independence. Amjad, who sought an arranged marriage for his daughter Amina, in *Borderline*, confesses that 'the day Churchill died, that winter, the English neighbours in Ealing came to us. We watched his funeral. You see he was our man too. You trusted things here though they fell down sometimes' (in *Outskirts*, 166).

But this is Amjad speaking posthumously, via a journalist's cassette. He died without seeing his daughter get married. His wife has now returned alone to Pakistan. Amjad and Churchill both represent a fading world order which is no more secure or ballast-supplying than the map of London which Danny draws for Rafi in *Sammy and Rosie Get Laid* but which soon becomes smudged and useless in the rain. This launderette is both the old edifice – and, in a sense, the old world – which is axed out of existence during Johnny's lusty refitting of Churchill's. Kureishi seems to imply that if there's to be any English regeneration, any possibility of recapturing a glory and swagger epitomized by the selfless bravery last seen in the Battle of Britain, it will only come through the homosexual pairing of a gauche Paki and a fascist sympathizer who both reject their ethnic and subcultural obligations and, in doing so, provide an eyebrow-raising recipe for national rejuvenation: in short, through sodomy, miscegenation and right-wing financial acuity.

By bringing discrete and seemingly disconnected elements into close quarters, juxtaposition and collage often create a rather surreal effect. In Kureishi's work, the borders, hinterlands and loci that people maintain within the capital are knocked sideways, dissolved and transformed into something unreal. Again, part of the impetus for such a technique stems from an aspect of 1960s pop culture: 'the first lesson of LSD was that reality was more evanescent and fugitive than most of us imagined for much of the time' (*Faber Book of Pop*, xviii).

Kureishi uses a form of surreal, psychedelic juxtaposition to more heartwarming and utopian effect in *My Beautiful Launderette*. Here, the all-new 'Powders' is within minutes of opening its doors for the first time. The advance publicity has been so successful that customers line the streets outside. Some peer through the glass. What they see bewilders them: Nasser and his mistress, Rachel, waltz across the launderette floor, caught up in their own amatory world, impervious to the watching hordes. Nasser, unlike the reader/viewer, can't see that all the time he's been dancing, Omar and Johnny have been '*making love vigorously, enjoying themselves thoroughly*' in the back room of the launderette (85).

In its conjunction of music, dancing, and guiltless sex, this scene combines a certain charming optimism with lyrical good humour. So there's a thrill of recognition from the audience when Omar and Johnny are briefly spotted circulating at one of Rosie's parties in Kureishi's next screenplay. Similarly, during one of their loved-up promenades in *The Black Album*, Shahid and Deedee find themselves in an Islington record shop poring over bootleg tapes of Charlie Hero, Karim's idol in *The Buddha of Suburbia*!

In refusing to confine his characters to one particular text, Kureishi's work illuminates one of the traditional features of London life – its ability to thrust people from different backgrounds and social spheres into sometimes fractious, sometimes harmonious co-existence. London isn't an organic community. On the contrary, it's a restless, clamorous agglomeration of exiles, migrants and refugees from suburbia and the sub-continent alike. In this respect, juxtaposition and collage are the ideal aesthetic modes for incarnating this higgledy-piggledy commotion of a metropolis.

A large part of London's appeal, like that of all major cities, is the promise it holds out for unfettered sexual activity. New arrivals in the capital have few friends or contacts to oversee their activities. They're likely to have travelled far from the parish or country in which they were born and brought up: parents can't lay down the law to them; gossiping neighbours and local communities can no longer keep a vigilant eye; schoolteachers and friends can't dogmatize or apply peer pressure on them. The lack of these forms of socialization can lead to a sense of anomie, of loneliness and isolation. Writers such as Rhys and Selvon have described at length the anxieties that follow the weakening of community and the loss of social vertebration.

Yet the absence of order and the freedom from constraint can also be liberating. Pop culture, in particular, has thrived on and celebrated these new licenses. A traditional reason for migrating to the city has been to exploit its possibilities for economic empowerment. Pop, rather than adopt such a Dick Whittington attitude, takes a different approach. Cherishing the opportunity the city allows for sloughing off one's old, 'square', socially-constricted self, it doesn't care very much for office culture, the weekly wage or for the life of the commuter. It privileges randomness, appetency, and sexual hedonism. Many of the pop stars I've already mentioned were well-fêted examples of incoming Londoners who chose to revel in the creative and sexual possibilities that the capital allowed: it was at Indica Books and Gallery off Duke Street in London that John Lennon met his Oriental soulmate, Yoko Ono; it was in London that Mick Jagger bedded women such as Marsha Hunt; and it was only in London where the young Jimi Hendrix could escape both the stylistic and sexual segregation that American culture in the 1960s imposed upon him.

Adolescents born outside London in the 1960s grew up listening to pop music on illicit pirate stations and sneaking in underaged to their local cinemas to gawp at a naked Julie Christie or a blissed-out Mick Jagger. The city became, in their collective imagination, the only place where they could, as Karim says, 'live always this intensely: mysticism, alcohol, sexual promise, clever people and drugs' (15). Kureishi has written that living in the suburbs triggered Gulf Syndrome, 'a dangerous psychological cocktail consisting of ambition, suppressed excitement, bitterness and sexual longing' ('Erotic Politicians and Mullahs', 144).

Although Karim and Ravi in *Borderline* view the prospect of living in London with tumescent anticipation, Kureishi doesn't sentimentalize sexual relations within the capital. One example of this is the high number of his characters who have blotched, disfigured bodies: Rafi's body is a 'geography of suffering' after his stomach, chest and back have been criss-crossed with scars from innumerable operations (*Sammy and Rosie*, 35); near the end of *My Beautiful Laundrette* Rachel reveals her 'blotched, marked' stomach to her lover, Nasser (105); in *The Buddha of Suburbia*, Eva undergoes a mastectomy; in the same novel, Changez, Jamila's arranged husband, is obese and has a withered arm; in *London Kills Me*, Clint's body is so cracked and eczematic that he never stops scratching.

These examples encompass characters of widely differing ages, genders and races. Despite their bodies ebbing and deteriorating, all these people are both eager to engage – and capable of doing so – in vigorous sexual activity. There's a clear parallel here with Kureish's portrayal of London's wilting landscape. I showed earlier how he homes in on the capital's underbelly, its squats, rundown pubs, dangerous Bengali estates and battered motorway arches, in order to prove that economic disenfranchisement and low social standing don't preclude creativity, energy and newer, more contingent forms of urban community. Similarly, Kureishi's depiction of his characters' flawed bodies suggests that imperfection and deformity needn't entrap or sexually restrict human beings. London's inner city may have been neglected during the 1980s, its social and economic fabric increasingly left to ruin, its inhabitants further disabled by the rundown in local government. But, for Kureishi, the fact that both corporeal and geographic landscapes are scarred and riddled merely strengthens his resolve to emphasize their vital resilience.

Bodies aren't always associated with handicap or disfigurement in Kureishi's work. Often they're symbols for the multiplicitous pleasures and temptations which urban life offers. ' "Karim," ' commands Marlene in *The Buddha of Suburbia*, ' "I want you to put some ice up my cunt" ' (204). As well as being crammed with frozen water, the body becomes decorable (women in both *Outskirts* and *Sammy and Rosie* have their buttocks tattooed with the letter 'W' so that when they bend down their male partners see – and think! – WOW); the body is also a palette of exquisite pain (Charlie has hot wax dripped on his penis).

Kureishi's half-Pakistani background lends a particular piquancy to this fascination with flesh. Frontal displays and public discussions of sexual gratification have long been taboo in Asian culture. Throughout the diaspora, millions of readers have grown up reading coyly titillating Asian film magazines which are studded with quote breaks from up and coming Hindi starlets who proclaim, 'I will show 20% more than Rifi, but 15% less than Bobby'.

And so, given that sex scenes, explicit language and nudity are totally forbidden, Kureishi's account of Tania swishing her breasts before a startled Zaki during *My Beautiful Laundrette*, and Jamila's intercrural voracity in *The Buddha of Suburbia*, aren't merely descriptive, but provocative assaults on the sensibilities of his more delicate Asian audiences.

These examples show how Kureishi's women desire at least as much as they are desired. In many of his sex scenes – Eva on the garden bench during *Buddha*, Rachel with Nasser in his car garage, Anna at the beginning of *Sammy and Rosie* – women are on top, the active partners, taking the lead role.

Tania's mammary display is also one of many scenes in Kureishi's work where exhibitionism and voyeurism play a large and visible role. Other instances include Omar eavesdropping on his uncle having sex in *My Beautiful Laundrette*; Karim watching his father and his future stepmother, Eva, make love in her garden near the start of *The Buddha of Suburbia*; Vivia and Rani's aggressively self-conscious lesbian clinching before Rafi in *Sammy and Rosie Get Laid*. Karim justifies watching his friend, Charlie, being tortured by a New York prostitute on the following grounds: 'How educational it could be! What knowledge of caresses, positions, attitudes, could be gleaned from practical example!' (254).

The word 'educational' is well chosen. It bears exactly the right connotations of didacticism, wilful provocation, and of wanting to 'epater les bourgeoisie'. More important than shocking first generation Asians, Kureishi's work during the second half of the 1980s was written against a background of what he felt was a Government-sponsored rise in narrow-minded homophobia and sexual repression. Individual examples included Margaret Thatcher's call for a return to Victorian values; the vilification of the Greater London Council by both the Conservative party and press for funding, in addition to other 'loony Left' organizations, various gay and lesbian groups; the introduction of Section 28 of the 1988 Local Government Act which forbade local authorities, at the risk of prosecution, from promoting homosexuality. Kureishi was not alone in attacking such measures. Bruce Robinson, director of *Withnail and I* (1986), was once asked why so many British films of the 1980s depicted homosexuality. He replied, 'because we're living in more and more repressive times, and of its nature the people who make films are people who are anti the repression' (Higgins, 252).

Another instance of London providing an accommodating arena for sexual harmony occurs in *Sammy and Rosie Get Laid*. At one and the same time, Danny and Rosie, Sammy and his girlfriend Anna, and Rafi and Alice are all shown fucking. The first pair are found in Danny's caravan which lies on a stretch of waste land that's soon to be redeveloped; the second pair lie on the roof of Anna's arty studio; the third pair occupy a crumbling bedroom in an expensive North London mansion. Between them, these six people represent a very wide social spectrum. Danny is an itinerant and hustler; Anna, a photographer; Sammy, a businessman; Rafi, a former Government cabinet minister. They come from different generations – Danny could be Rafi's son. They have conflicting political views – Alice's old-fashioned Conservatism is at odds with Danny's street-based radicalism. The latter's also black, Rafi and Sammy are Pakistani, and the others white. Collectively, they cover a cultural range the width of which can only ever be found in cities like London. And here they all are '*in energetic, tender and ecstatic climax*', welded together by Kureishi in a '*COLLAGE OF COPULATION IMAGES*' (44).

One part of the sexual triptych above involves Sammy and Anna making love on a roof which overlooks a London motorway whilst a helicopter whirrs over their heads. Similarly, in *Buddha*, as Jamila commits adultery with Karim, the windows in her flat are open 'drenching the atmosphere in car fumes and the uproar of the unemployed arguing in the street' (107). These examples show that, for Kureishi, a preoccupation with sex neither entails individualism, nor a neglect of the social realm, that world outside the windows of rutting lovers.

Whether heterosexual or homosexual, male-centred or female-slanted, onanistic or orgiastic, in Kureishi's work London is both witness to, and an active fomentor of, mass sexual activity. It allows for a vast range of people to meet each other, it repudiates the coyness and caution of suburbia, it abounds with individuals who all arrived thirsting for novelty, excitement and new experiences. It's hardly surprising, then, if London itself becomes sexualized. One of the most memorable passages in *The Black Album* involves Shahid travelling along the Northern Line only to be seized by a fantasy which he recalls Deedee had masturbated to:

> She would be walking around the city in high heels, lipstick and a transparent dress, her nipples and cunt visible, not being touched, but looked at. And as she walked she would watch men watching her; and as they masturbated she would stroke herself. (103)

The language and imagery may be lurid, but the basic emotions underlying this fantasy aren't so unusual in Kureishi's writing. At one level, Deedee's self-exposure is a response to the newly experienced license and liberty that the city affords newcomers. She's being an exhibitionist to a degree that she could never have been in buttoned-up Bromley. At the same time, her exposure bears another connotation: she's putting herself, metaphorically speaking, in the hands of the city which she trusts, stripping away those layers of decorum and respectability that Kureishi believes are more often sought by those who live outside the city. Deedee can't be harmed because bystanders may not touch her. This suggests a degree of idealism that's further borne out by Kureishi's comment that the sexed-up platform of Baker Street Station 'was Arcadia itself' (103).

The men aren't distinguished or individuated. They stand for London itself. The fact that they masturbate on seeing Deedee indicates how London has traditionally thrived on, and been stimulated by, each new wave of incomers. Its enduring vitality has always depended on the willingness of arrivants to use London as an arena for heightened commercial, creative and sexual energy. The sheer momentum and thrill of living in London inspires its peoples to hustle, dream and overcome the limitations that prejudice, penury and timidity create. And, as they do so, London is itself sustained and constituted by their energies. It's a reciprocal relationship: London comes – because Deedee came to London.

One day, in *London Kills Me*, Clint's posse decide to leave the capital. They need a break, a day out. Clint himself has no job, no home and little money. He can't even steal the pair of shoes he needs to find paid work. He's scared that the drug-dealer, Mr. G, is going to pay him back for the previous night's failed business deal. So the posse leave for the countryside where they'll visit Clint's mother. They hope to escape the noise, the fumes, the endless pressure of city life. They want some fresh air, and they want to be revivified. They fail. As soon as they disembark from the bus onto the country lane they're 'a little bewildered, looking lost' (49). Clint's mum, Lily, isn't pleased to see them. Nor is her husband, Stone, who abuses them for being jobless 'slaves of sensation' (59). An argument breaks out. Clint starts tussling with his stepfather.

The posse return home. It's been a miserable, shitty day. But it has allowed Clint to come to a mushroom-fuelled insight about the kind of life he truly values. And it isn't one he'll find in the country where 'the people are sly and cunning and ignorant . . . I know what I want to do. Get back to London and be with the only people for me, having adventures . . .' (51).

It's a telling admission. Clint is hapless, dependent, and near the bottom of the capital's social and economic ladder. In this sense, London is killing him, grinding him down. But, for all that, Clint finds life in the capital preferable to the corrosive mean-mindedness of the countryside from which he's just fled. London, at least, is full of action, possibility, adrenalizing happenstance – it's good, it 'kills' him.

It's this toleration of – and even revelling in – the more fractured, fallen aspects of London life that distinguishes Kureishi from other Asian and Caribbean writers. His characters harry, lope and arterialize their ways through the capital with queer abandon. They don't pine for the order and mature certainties that writers from Gronniosaw onwards sought. London, for Kureishi's characters, is something of a spree, a passport to mobility, a chance to rid themselves of their cossetted, comfy suburban pasts. Consequently, they're not interested, as Naipaul was, in 'finding the centre'. Such a notion was more poignant for pre-Independence writers who'd grown up believing – and being taught – that they were on the outskirts, the margins of English culture. Kureishi was born into a relatively affluent family in snug Bromley and didn't suffer from this cultural cringe. On the contrary, he values London not for the stability and assurances it offers, but for its disruptions and upheavals, qualities missing in the suburbs. London is still a centre for Kureishi, but one, he hopes, where things fall apart, where the centre cannot hold.

Compared to previous Asian writers, Kureishi's is startlingly relaxed about the changes the capital might wreak on his personality. For many immigrants London is an interlude, a city they inhabit reluctantly for purely financial reasons. They don't come to the metropolis to refashion themselves. Money – not hybridity – impels them. Their lives are petrified as they cleave dogmatically to their memories, the values and norms on which they and their parents were weaned. Sour and tetchy, timid and ashamed, refusing to acknowledge or embrace the merits of their new environments, such immigrants prove that geographical dislocation doesn't necessarily transform people. Gender, age, politics and, most importantly, individual disposition all shape (outsiders') perceptions of the city. Kureishi's celebration of self-shifting identifies a particular way of looking at the city, one not ubiquitous but increasingly common, especially amongst those second generation children wearied by the rigidities and strictures of domestic lore.

The traditional Hindu concern for self purity led many nineteenth- and early twentieth-century Indian writers to fear that London would muddy or canker their souls. T. Ramakrishna even delayed leaving for England because his mother feared he would become a 'walking corpse', a living dead body, a being socially and religiously lost to her, to our family and clan' (3). When he does finally arrive in London, he vows to remain ' "untainted," as pure a Hindu as I was when I first saw the light of day' (5). In *The Buddha of Suburbia*, Karim's father Haroon, although a Muslim, experienced a comically concretized form of Ramakrishna's anxieties when he came to England in the 1950s: 'no one had told him the English didn't wash regularly because the water was so cold' (24). Kureishi, however, associates such talk of cleanliness with the kind of social hygiene that led property developers in *Sammy and Rosie* and the fundamentalist Riaz in *The Black Album* to seek to overturn the demotic variety and deregulated bustle of the capital. Characters like Karim and Shahid believe in the plasticity of self. They came to London precisely in order to pursue the skewing and pollution of identity.

It's perhaps most useful to see Kureishi as part of a class of artists which, following the post-war flight from London to the suburbs, the ensuing de-industrialization of the capital, and the emergence of a much-maligned and much-feared inner city, has sought to reclaim the creative and vibrant possibilities of urban life. This wasn't a project that planners, property developers, broadsheet commentators or Government ministers seemed either aware of or interested in. Rather, it was the achievement of a certain social cluster – dropouts, artists, filmmakers, students, pop musicians (like Bowie and The Beatles) – whose clubs, fanzines, cafés, and dress codes all embody the polyphony and miscegenation of peoples, energies and ideas that have helped keep London as the (pop) cultural capital of Europe. It's this idea of a creative, 24-hour city which offers so many opportunities for federation and experimentation, and which is forever morphing, pulsing, forever young that excites Kureishi and which he's chosen to explore in his work. In doing so, he's become perhaps the first – and certainly the best and most important – Asian chronicler of London.

Works Cited

Gilroy, P., 1993. *Small Acts: Thoughts on the Politics of Black Cultures*, London: Serpent's Tail.

Higgins, P. (ed.), 1993. *A Queer Reader*, London: Fourth Estate.

Hobhouse, M., February 1890. 'London Sketched by an Indian Pen', *The Indian Magazine* Vol. 21 No. 230, 61–73.

Kureishi, H., Spring 1986. 'Erotic Politicians and Mullahs', *Granta* No. 17, 139–51.

——, 1986. *My Beautiful Laundrette*, London: Faber.

——, 1988. *Sammy and Rosie Get Laid*, London: Faber.
——, 2 September 1988. 'Finishing The Job', *New Statesman and Society*, 19–24.
——, 1990. *The Buddha of Suburbia*, London: Faber.
——, 1991. *London Kills Me*, London: Faber.
——, 1992. *Outskirts and Other Plays* [inc. *The King and Me, Outskirts, Borderline, Birds of Passage*], London: Faber.
——, 1995. *The Black Album*, London: Faber.
——, 1997. *Love in a Blue Time*, London: Faber.
——, 1998. *Intimacy*, London: Faber.
——, 1998. *My Son the Fanatic*, London: Faber.
——, 1999. *Sleep With Me*, London: Faber.
——, & Jon Savage (eds.), 1995. *The Faber Book of Pop*, London: Faber.
Meadows, D., 1988. *Nattering in Paradise: A Word from the Suburbs*, London: Simon and Schuster.
Mellor, D., 1993. *The Sixties Art Scene In London*, London: Phaidon Press.
Ramakrishna, T., 1915. *My Visit to the West*, London: T. Fisher Unwin.
Thomson, E. and D. Gutman (eds.), [1993] 1995. *The Bowie Companion*, London: Sidgwick and Jackson.

Your rash song. That will go. That will go.

Notes on Contributors

Laura Chrisman teaches at Sussex University and has published widely on postcolonial theory, black writing, South African literatures and British imperial culture. She co-edited *Colonial Discourse and Postcolonial Theory: A Reader* (1993) and her monograph, *Empire and Opposition: South Africa and Imperial Culture*, is forthcoming from Oxford University Press. She is currently Visiting Associate Professor at Brown University.

Vilashini Cooppan is Assistant Professor of Comparative Literature at Yale University, where she teaches postcolonial studies, the literatures of slavery and literary theory. She has published on postcolonial feminism and postcolonial uses of psychoanalysis, and is currently working on a book, exploring figurations of race and nation in postcolonial writing.

Fernando Coronil is Associate Professor of Anthropology and History at the University of Michigan and Research Associate of IDEA, Universidad Simón Bolivar, Venezuela. He has written extensively on contemporary historical transformations in Latin America. His most recent publications include *The Magical State: Nature, Money and Modernity in Venezuela* (University of Chicago Press), the Introduction to Fernando Ortiz's *Cuban Counterpoint: Tobacco and Sugar*, and 'Beyond Occidentalism: Towards Non-Imperial Geohistorical Categories'.

Benita Parry is Honorary Professor in the Department of English and Comparative Literature at Warwick University. She is the author of *Delusions and Discoveries: India in the British Imagination* (revised edition 1998, first published 1972), *Conrad and Imperialism* (1984) and numerous essays in the area of colonial discourse theory and postcolonial studies. She co-edited and contributed to the volume, *Cultural Readings of Imperialism: Edward Said and the Gravity of History* (1997).

Lawrence Phillips is a Ph.D. student in English at Goldsmiths College, University of London. His research is concerned with a comparative reading of the 'South Sea' writings of Robert Louis Stevenson and Jack London. His engagement with postcolonial theory includes an essay, 'Lost in Space: Siting/Citing the Inbetween of Homi Bhabha's *The Location of Culture*, in *Scrutiny 2* Vol. 3 No. 1 (1998).

Gautam Premnath is completing a Ph.D. in English at Brown University entitled 'Colour Bar: Race and Realism in Post-Imperial Britain'. His research interests include twentieth-century British and Caribbean literatures, and theories of postcoloniality and diaspora. He is a member of the editorial collective of *Ghadar*, the journal of the Forum of the Indian Left.

Ato Quayson is a Fellow of Pembroke College, Lecturer in English and Director of the African Studies Centre at Cambridge University. He is the author of *Strategic Transformations in Nigerian Writing* (1997) and is currently working on a book about postcolonialism for Polity Press.

Sukhdev Sandhu is Junior Research Fellow in English at Wolfson College, Oxford University.

Tim Watson teaches in the English department at Montclair State University. His work has appeared in, or is forthcoming in, the journals *ARIEL*, *Diaspora*, *Jouvert*, and *Postmodern Culture*. He is currently working on a book entitled *The Sun Also Sets: Transatlantic Cultures and the End of the British Empire*.